Speak for Me, Mom

Andreas Dresp (1/24/1970–6/11/1989)

Speak for Me, Mom

A murder, a trial, and a mother's enduring love

A MEMOIR

Christine Wolf

Androscoggin Press
2023

Androscoggin Press, West Kennebunk, Maine
Copyright @ 2023 by Christine Wolf

Wolf, Christine, 1945–
Speak for Me, Mom: A murder, a trial, and a mother's enduring love / Christine Wolf
Original trade paperback ISBN-13: 978-1-7329471-4-6
E-book ISBN-13: 978-1-7329471-5-3
Library of Congress Control Number: 2023904301

This book is a memoir. It reflects the author's recollection of events to the best of her knowledge. Dialogue from jury selection and courtroom trial testimony is based on the actual court transcripts. Dialogue outside the courtroom setting has been re-created from the author's memory. Some names and identifying characteristics of people have been changed to protect their privacy.

Edited by Jennifer Huston Schaeffer at White Dog Editorial.

Cover photograph by Elaine Giles.

Book & cover design Deb Tremper at Six Penny Graphics.

Tom Petty, "Free Fallin'," track 1 on *Full Moon Fever*, released April 24, 1989, MCA Records.

For further information and permissions approval or to order copies of this book, go to www.christinewolfauthor.com.

First Printing, 2023
Printed in the United States of America

This work is dedicated to my beloved
sons, Andreas and Tom Dresp.

In memory of my mother, Frieda; my mother's brother,
Paul, who was killed during World War II; my maternal
grandparents, who went to their graves with the pain of not
knowing where nor how their son, Paul, had been buried; and
my father, Stefan, who, after losing several family members
during World War II, lost his grandson to murder.

Contents

Foreword

I met Christina, as she's known to friends and family, shortly after I arrived in Boston from Venezuela. Though we'd never met in our hometown of Maracaibo, I had heard mutual friends there speak fondly of her. I was particularly pleased to meet Christina a week after I started my job at a counseling center in the Greater Boston area and to discover that we worked just a few blocks away from each other and in the same field, she as a clinical social worker and I as a psychologist. It seemed to me incredibly good luck or synchronicity. It was the spring of 1989, just weeks before Andreas, Christina's nineteen-year-old son, was murdered. Neither of us knew then how much our lives would soon change.

Over the years, I have witnessed Christina struggle to make sense of the senseless. How can a mother cope with the murder of her son? At first, she kept detailed journals of her experiences and feelings. Much of what she wrote was not only extremely painful but keenly insightful. Gradually, some of her pages morphed into a draft of this book, which I first read in 1999. That draft had a profound impact on me as a clinical psychologist working with inner-city families, helping me become more compassionate and empathic toward the needs of parents whose children had been murdered. Christina's rough draft gave me an invaluable tool for connecting with such families. Instead of compartmentalizing my feelings as I would've preferred to do, I was able to stay with the pain and use my feelings to connect with the parents—just as I had learned from Christina.

As with that first draft, I read the final version of this book in one weekend. This time, I felt Christina's pain even more vividly. To have a child murdered is unimaginable to any parent. But as the father of a son in his early twenties—a young man full of promise, who grew up in Belmont just like Andreas—Christina's emotional and raw writing particularly hit home and spoke directly to my heart. Once I started reading, I couldn't stop. The judge, jurors, and accused murderer came to life on the page, and I became outraged as the story unfolded. I wanted to cry or scream or even put the book down and step away. It was as if I were in the courtroom with Christina.

Speak for Me, Mom has touched and moved me and brought the inconceivable closer to home. I know that I cannot live my life with eyes closed; murder can touch not just my neighbor's family but also my own. Openly discussing murder and youth violence is one step in the right direction of learning to prevent it. With this book, Christina offers us her tears. In doing so, together we can start processing the unbearable pain and unthinkable horror of losing a child. There is much pain in this life, and we must confront it if we're going to grow and heal. This book left me feeling thankful for all I have.

Martin J. La Roche, PhD
Author and Associate Professor of Psychology at Harvard Medical School
Director of Mental Health Training at Boston Children's Hospital at Martha Eliot

"Be indignant and be angry at what has happened to Andreas. God does not will such madness. God calls us to life and wants wholeness for us."

—The late Reverend Charles Foreman of King's Chapel, Boston, from his graveside eulogy for Andreas Dresp, June 14, 1989

Preface

On June 11, 1989, my nineteen-year-old son, Andreas, was murdered. I wanted to scream over and over for the world to hear, "Andreas was killed! Andreas was killed!" but I couldn't. Instead of screaming out loud, I screamed inside. Days later, I took a pencil, placed it on a sheet of paper, and let my hand move in whatever way it needed.

As the days passed without hearing Andreas open our back door and walk up the stairs, my heart was struck with the reality that I would never see him again, never hear his voice again, never be able to touch him again. That feeling of "never again," tore through me in the deepest place of my being. Holding on to my pencil and journaling helped me hang on to life.

I soon began writing letters to Andreas, which helped me feel that he was still with me. Knowing I could not escape the reality that he would never return home, I asked myself, *Who am I now? Am I no longer the mother of two sons?*

Six months after Andreas's death, to help prepare myself for the first Christmas without him, I attended a traumatic death support group in nearby Somerville, Massachusetts. It was there that I met a mother, about my age, whose seventeen-year-old son had been killed at a party six years earlier. Our group facilitator, Bette Spear, had invited the woman to talk to our newly bereaved group about how she had survived her first Christmas without her son. Though her voice cracked with emotion as she addressed us, it surprised me that she was able to speak so coherently, hold down a job, and take care of her remaining son. As she spoke her last word, I stood up and automatically went to thank her. Teary-eyed, we embraced, and I felt welcomed into a club to which I had never imagined I'd belong. Afterward, I drove home hoping to find Andreas resting on his bed.

A few months later, I began to attend the newly established OMEGA Homicide Support Group, also led by Bette Spear in Somerville. It was there where, over many years, I met other mothers, fathers, daughters, sons, sisters, and brothers of murder victims. In that group, we found a safe space to freely tell what had happened to our loved ones, talk about our encounters with the criminal justice system, cry, often sob, and express our rage. Despite the continued pain, we were also able to laugh and share thoughts about what we might do in memory of our loved ones. Different members had different plans; some created scholarship funds in memory of their daughter or son, while others worked to help create the Garden of Peace in Boston, in memory of murder victims in our state. To honor the memory of my own son, I was called to give Andreas a voice by writing this book.

In 1992, three years after the murder of my son, I began working at a city community health center. Drawn to the opportunity to serve patients from diverse backgrounds, I soon discovered that many, if not most, had experienced trauma in various forms: war, homicide, community violence, domestic abuse, economic hardship, and sexual abuse. Hearing about these patients' experiences and reflecting on my own background as a child of German World War II refugees led me to go back and take a closer look at my journals. As a psychotherapist and mother, I felt driven to better understand what was happening inside me. How was the murder of my son affecting my sense of identity? I became curious to understand how grief following the murder of a loved one felt different from other forms of bereavement I had experienced.

As I continued to journal and write letters to Andreas, I began to feel the urge to turn what I'd written into a memoir focused specifically on my thoughts, feelings, and emotions in the wake of my son's murder and my experience of attending the trial. Over the years, whenever I put the manuscript aside and tried to go on with my life, I felt a deep restlessness inside, as if Andreas was telling me, "Mom, you have to tell our story—what happened to me *and* to you." I listened to that feeling, and when it became clear that I owed it to Andreas to give him a voice outside our family, I finally found the courage to share with others my experience as the mother of a murdered son.

Had Andreas been the last homicide victim since 1989, perhaps I would not have considered publishing this story. Sadly, there have been many more sons and daughters killed since then. I learned that painful truth—not just from listening to the news or reading statistics—but by continuing to attend the homicide support group for over ten years. As a clinical social worker, I learned about this reality from my patients as well. Many of them had lost family members to homicide. I've also felt the anguish of parents who fear their sons will commit a violent crime or become the victim of one.

For all these reasons, I felt a strong need to bear witness to the indelible pain homicide causes the families and friends of the victims. To this day, I still ask myself, *Why was Andreas forced to give up his life? Can there be any meaning to his cruel death?* My purpose in writing this memoir has been to make some sense of it all and raise awareness—particularly among adolescent boys and young men—of the consequences that stem from acts of violence. Everyone—especially young people—needs to realize that a murder has victims. Murder is too often portrayed in movies, TV shows, and video games as entertainment. But real-life violence victimizes, traumatizes, and indelibly scars living, breathing people, leaving their lives forever changed.

I'm also publishing our story to show how keeping a journal helped me express and process my grief and pain. Writing letters to Andreas offered solace and gave voice to my overwhelming emotions. I can now say that it was the act of holding a pen in my hand

and letting it scribble all over the pages of my journal that helped me survive such a traumatic event. As time passed and I began sharing my writing with others, I discovered a force deep within that helped hold me together amidst the desolation. I often asked myself, *Is it you, Andreas? You and God?*

When I wasn't writing, that force often called me to take long walks without a planned destination. Sometimes while walking, I sensed a dim light breaking through the darkness in my heart, like a flickering candle. On other days, I felt pulled to look at a certain tree, feel the sturdiness of its trunk, and listen to its rustling leaves. Sometimes the leaves began to glow as if they were aware of my pain and were trying to comfort me.

More than thirty years have passed since Andreas last walked down our back steps to go out with his friends and never returned home. And although I still feel the urge to visit with Andreas at the cemetery, I no longer write to him. Now when I stand at his grave under the immense shade cast by the grown katsura trees, I stare at my son's full name—Andreas Peter Dresp—and the two dates—January 24, 1970 and June 11, 1989—inscribed on the aging, gray stone and shake my head, thinking about all we've both missed in the years since his death.

PART I

I stumble through tangled darkness,
trip over heavy rocks.
Thorns prick my skin.

Where are you, Andreas!?
Where did you go?

I don't leave a single stone
that reflects light unturned.
I gaze at every corner, at each road,
at open spaces, closed buildings,
trying to find you.

I touch the warm path,
the damp earth, the fresh grass
you may have walked on.

Where are you!?
Where did you go?

CHAPTER 1

June 1989

Returning from the hospital, I collapsed on the living room rug. Vivid images of Andreas taking his first steps on that same rug mingled with images of his size 10 feet in his blue slippers. The appearance of our friends, coworkers, and neighbors that Sunday afternoon in June interrupted those images. I lifted my body to embrace our visitors and repeated over and over, "Andreas was killed. Andreas was killed." But each time, the floor pulled me back.

My husband, Robert, remained standing and was able to talk to our guests. The smell of lasagna and the sound of hushed voices filled our rooms. My body, despite invitations from my friends to lie down on the sofa, remained curled up on the floor. I waited for Andreas, our nineteen-year-old-son, even though I knew he would never again step on our living room rug. Never again. Never again.

"Christine, stand up now," Robert said quietly as he reached his hand toward me. "Mr. Brooks from the funeral home is here. He wants to talk to us."

I was barely able to get off the floor, but Robert helped me stand up. Confused, I looked at the slender, middle-aged stranger in a gray suit and bow tie. I knew that the father of one of Andreas's friends was familiar with a local funeral home and had asked the owner to come to our house to help, but I didn't want to see him in our living room. Robert offered Mr. Brooks a seat in the black rocking chair. My heart cracked as his body reached the chair's worn cushion. Clear images of me holding Andreas as a baby and rocking him to sleep where the funeral director now sat flashed through my mind. I heard myself scream without a sound, *How can he sit in that chair? Get off! Go away!*

Mr. Brooks bombarded Robert and me with questions. "Do you have a good recent picture of Andreas that I can take along?"

How dare this stranger ask for a picture of our son! "What do you need it for?" I cried, my voice shaking in disbelief.

"We need it so we can reconstruct his face as close as possible to how he looked in life," he replied in a flat, measured tone.

"I don't understand! What do you mean 'reconstruct'? Why would you need to do that?" My stomach lurched and a sense of dread spread through me.

Stone-faced, he ignored my questions and asked, "Do you have any special clothes you want your son to wear?"

"I am *not* giving away Andreas's pants or shirts! I'm keeping them."

Mike and Todd, two of Andreas's best friends, offered to go shopping for the clothes Andreas would be buried in.

As he prepared to leave, Mr. Brooks told us, "I'll see you tomorrow morning at the funeral home so you can pick out a coffin."

I glared at Mr. Brooks as he turned around to go down our front stairs. Then the floor once again pulled me down.

As daylight began to fade, I stopped hearing familiar voices. The footsteps of our friends, neighbors, and colleagues disappeared. I didn't know where my twenty-year-old-son, Tom, had gone. I'd last seen him when he came home with us from the hospital. A haunted silence filled our rooms, but a thunderous storm tore through my body. At one point, Kristi, who lived below us on the first floor of our two-family house, appeared. She bent down silently, her kind face close to mine. Softly taking my hand, she opened my palm, placed a pill on it, and whispered, "Take this. Your doctor prescribed it for you." Then she lifted my head, placed a glass of water to my lips, tucked a pillow under my head, and left.

Soon after, Robert's deep voice emanated from the silence. "Christine, can you come to bed now?"

"I can't. I'll stay here!" I cried out. *How can I go to sleep as if nothing has happened? How can life go on in its usual pattern? It makes no sense. Everything has changed.* How can I sleep in the same bed that faces the playground near where Andreas was just killed? How can I do that to my son?

I remained on the living room floor that night to honor Andreas. Knowing I would never again feel the warmth of his gentle presence, in the darkness a stream of fleeting images sped by in my mind's eye as if on a fast-moving screen: Andreas as a baby, a toddler, school-aged, until the images slowed and lingered on the previous evening—the last time I saw my son alive.

He was walking through the living room with his lower body wrapped in a bath towel. With his muscular legs, long and sturdy, and his feet in blue slippers, Andreas carried his portable stereo in one hand. He made his way to the bathroom to shower before the image changes.

The next thing I saw was him standing in the corner of our kitchen next to the wooden pull-down ironing board. He was intently focused as he moved the steaming iron across the fabric of two newly bought shirts. When he noticed me, he looked up and grinned, showing me his sweet smile. Softly he asked, "Mom, which one looks better on me?"

Deciding on the green-striped shirt, he thrust an arm into each sleeve, buttoned the front, and tucked the shirttails neatly into his jeans. His freshly scrubbed face shined and the golden eagle pendant hanging from his neck reflected the depth and warmth of his dark eyes. His hair, which was still damp from the shower, fell in light waves across his forehead. I caught a whiff of his cherished Polo cologne as he passed me on his way toward our back stairs. It is this image of Andreas rushing happily out the door and down our wooden steps to our driveway that stayed with me in the darkness until my body succumbed to sleep.

—∿—

The following day, as warm rays of early morning sunlight streamed through our living room windows, I saw myself lying on the floor. *Andreas, where are you? Where did you go? Why aren't you home yet?* My body had become a hollow cave from which my silent screams could not escape. Then a thought shook my whole being, *Andreas will never come home again. It's irreversible. This can't be! Please let me wake up, please, please.*

"Christine, we're here with you," a voice interrupted my waking nightmare.

I opened my eyes and saw Kathy and Sherry, my friends of more than twenty years, crawling toward me on the floor. I didn't know they'd spent the night sleeping on the nearby rug in the adjoining dining room. I stared at them in disbelief. The world as I knew it had ended, yet my friends were with me. But it wouldn't be long before they had to leave. It was Monday morning, and both had long commutes to their jobs from my home in Belmont, Massachusetts; Kathy worked in New Hampshire and Sherry on Cape Cod. When they left, I remained curled up on the floor, seeing only the images that flashed through my mind of the events that had unfolded at the hospital just over twenty-four hours before.

Robert and I had been alone in a dimly lit cubicle. I had rested on an empty stretcher as my husband sat beside me in a stiff-backed chair. By then, the emergency room had quieted. Fearfully awaiting news from the surgeon who was attending to Andreas's stab wound, I'd worried, *Where is Tom? He must've gone home with one of Andreas's friends*, I'd concluded.

Now the images changed quickly. The doctor in his white lab coat said, "Andreas's liver was critically damaged from the stab wound, and he's lost a lot of blood. He's being prepared for surgery right now. I'll let you know how he responds as soon as I can."

Maureen, Mike's mother and a nurse from Ireland, had come to sit with us in the ER cubicle for a while. She told us that her sister in Ireland was praying for the surgeon and for Andreas to make it through the operation.

When the doctor updated us following surgery, he said, "Andreas is resting. Now we need to wait and see how he responds." Hours later he returned, this time delivering his news in a softer voice. "Andreas's temperature is not coming up. His body is very cold. We're doing what we can, but if he survives, he'll need a liver transplant. He'll never be the same."

When the doctor said those words, my heart plummeted. It was like a sheet of ice painfully cutting through my body. I began to shiver and could feel Robert shaking next to me.

Later, when we were reunited with Tom, who we learned had spent the night all alone in a cubicle near us, a young woman led the three of us to the hospital's large dining hall. Julia, a family friend whom I'd met years before on the playground when Andreas was learning to walk, entered the stark, fluorescent-lit room. Her sorrowful face reflected the mixture of sadness and fear that we all felt. As she joined us at a vacant table, I noticed a group of young men standing on the other side of the cafeteria and watched as they removed their teal-colored scrub caps and surgical coats. *Are they the ones who just tried to save Andreas? Should I go over and ask them how Andreas is doing?*

A young woman brought each of us a tray with an English muffin and scrambled eggs. *When are they taking us to see Andreas?* I wondered. A short while later, the young woman returned and escorted Robert, Tom, and me down a long, harshly lit corridor. She stopped at a doorway and led us into an empty room. "The doctor will be right with you," she said before leaving. Within moments, the young doctor who'd kept us informed throughout the night walked in through the open door. I watched him closely, expecting him to gesture for us to follow him into another room so we could finally see Andreas.

How is Andreas going to look? I asked myself fearfully.

The doctor's voice was flat and devoid of any sign of emotion as he stoically told us, "Andreas suffered grave injuries. His liver was critically damaged when he was stabbed. We worked on him for hours, trying to repair the damage. We did everything we could, but I'm sorry to inform you that Andreas gave up his fight for life this morning at quarter past ten."

Andreas gave up his fight for life? The words hit me like a lightning bolt plunging me to the ground and reverberating through my soul. My body wrenched into a downward spiral toward an infinitely deep black hole as Robert and Tom crashed next to me on the cold vinyl floor. The most painful words I'd ever heard shattered the life I'd known, signaling that my life as a mother of two sons had abruptly ended. In that moment, I found myself in a disorienting void of utter darkness, as if lost in a frightening nightmare. Neither the doctor's words nor the frightening images they invoked would vanish. The nightmare was real.

In my state of confusion, I was surprised to see our downstairs neighbor Kristi suddenly appear above us, extending her arms and reaching to help the three of us stand to face the white-coated doctor. Julia entered and joined us in the center of the room. At that moment, as the stoic doctor took a quick breath, I thought to myself, *Now he'll tell us we can go in and see Andreas.* Instead, he said, "Somebody needs to go in and identify Andreas. It's a legal thing."

Has Andreas become an object that needs to be looked at and identified? This can't be! I want to go through that door and see Andreas, I silently screamed. *I want to go through that door!*

"What do you mean? We've waited to see him all night! We know him! What is there to identify?" I pleaded with the doctor. "Why don't we all go in? We *all* want to see him."

Without hesitation, the doctor continued, "Andreas no longer looks the same as he did the last time you saw him. I don't recommend that you go in to see him. I'm sure you want to remember him as he was in life. And because your son's death is the result of a crime, we need to let the coroner get in there now to do his job."

Please! We need to go in and see Andreas! Please . . . I need to touch him!

The doctor shifted his gaze toward Julia, who somehow knew what was being asked of her. Without a word but with a face full of sadness, Julia stepped away from us and slowly followed the doctor through the open door to identify Andreas. Standing motionless, Robert, Tom, and I looked to one another, speechless in our shock.

Just minutes later, Julia appeared at the doorway followed by the solemn-faced doctor. Pausing before fully entering the room, they stopped, and the doctor spoke to her in a hushed voice that the three of us couldn't hear. Then Julia approached me and said, "His legs felt strong and sturdy. I touched them. It felt good to do that."

My pleading eyes watched her lips move as she spoke, silently begging her to add, "I'll go in with you. I'll help you touch him too." But before such an offer could be made, my body reverberated with the memory of the authoritative tone of the doctor's voice saying, "I don't recommend that you go in to see him." Did his well-meaning advice silence my desperate need as a mother to touch Andreas just one more time, no matter how horrific his wounds were? Robert and Tom, their faces ashen, still stood facing me as if stuck to the floor. Their own longings to see Andreas could not find expression either.

With her eyes downcast, Julia quietly let us know that she would accompany us home. I watched as she slowly exited the door leading to the corridor of the hospital. Every fiber of my being told me to stay behind to sit with Andreas. I knew he needed his mother, father, and brother now. And we needed to be with him—to take his hand, stroke his forehead, tell him how much we all loved him. Instead, I mechanically fell in line with Robert and Tom as Julia led us through a maze of passageways and out of the hospital. As we exited onto the sidewalk, a force stronger than anything I've ever felt gripped my soul and tried to pull me back, back through the maze of corridors and back to

Andreas. But with every step toward our car, the car we had parked on the street when we were still a family of four, we moved further and further away from him.

Over time, I would come to realize that the doctors and nurses were doing their jobs as best they could throughout that long night, relying on their skill and training to try to save Andreas's life and then, when all efforts had failed, informing us of his death as factually and as devoid of emotion as possible. Yet no pastor was available at the hospital that Sunday morning to comfort us; no one suggested we sit down before we received the worst news of our lives. Going through the experience was shocking, and I will never understand why we weren't allowed to see Andreas and say a proper goodbye. That said, in retrospect, I now have more clarity regarding the medical staff's circumstances, and I often think about the impact Andreas's death likely had on them, particularly the surgeon who tried to save his life and would later be called to testify at the trial.

The sound of the doorbell ringing brought me back to our living room where my body remained on the rug. "Christine, Susan is here," Robert informed me as he came into the room. "You need to get ready. She's going to take us to the funeral home now."

With great effort, I got up and followed Robert downstairs to meet Susan, my close, longtime friend. We'd met years earlier at an adult carpentry class when Andreas and her son, Jason, were both three years old. We quickly discovered that we had a lot in common as young mothers who, in addition to caring for our sons, also had ambitions to study and improve our professional lives. Andreas, Tom, and Jason were close friends during their early years, and Susan and I spent much time together with the boys and each other, taking them sledding down the hills of our local golf club in winter and relishing the sounds of their youthful laughter drifting in through the open windows during the summer as they played basketball together in the driveway.

Soon we arrived at a large building painted a pale gray with white trim and black shutters. Although the modest sign by the road spelled out *Funeral Home* in neatly stenciled letters, it was obvious that the business, like so many in New England, occupied a building that had once been a stately private home. Before Andreas was killed, I'd never really noticed the place, even though I'd walked by it many times. Mr. Brooks, the man in the gray suit from the day before, greeted us at the entrance. I stared at his hands, wondering, *Have they touched Andreas? What does he feel like? How does he look?*

"Please come in and sit down," Mr. Brooks said respectfully. Spreading papers out neatly on a table in front of us, he continued, "These are the services we can provide, and these are the prices."

Susan, who sat between Robert and me, took the documents and tried to help us decide what we really needed. We stood and left the papers behind when Mr. Brooks led us into another room. Crossing the threshold, I quickly noticed the caskets lining the room's four walls. My legs became weak, and I could feel the floor beneath me shake as if we were in the midst of an earthquake. I managed to steady myself while Mr. Brooks explained the different types of caskets available. He showed us a variety of boxes—some made of shiny hardwood, others of dull metal—all lined with sage-green, pale pink, or periwinkle-blue satin. Each one had a tiny matching pillow. *Andreas has a queen-size bed waiting for him at home. His pillow is large and fluffy with a cotton cover. That's what he likes. Andreas cannot go into any of these boxes!*

"Which one would you like?" Mr. Brooks asked. "The advantages of a metal casket are . . ."

As he explained the differences between the various coffins, I felt lost. The overwhelming shock of the circumstances prevented me from comprehending the funeral director's words. *Where am I? Why is the room spinning? This can't be happening!*

"Andreas is very tall," Mr. Brooks continued. "I think this metal one would be large enough for him."

I glanced into the coffin and gave a silent nod of approval. His voice trembling, Robert turned to Mr. Brooks and said, "We'll take this one."

Susan, our constant guide, drove us to our next stop: the cemetery. *I want to go home. I want to be there when Andreas returns and this nightmare ends,* I silently protested. But the car kept moving toward the cemetery, to the place I didn't want to go. *I want to hug Andreas when he gets home. Where is Tom? I don't know where he is.*

Susan spoke to the receptionist at the cemetery's administrative office. Within minutes, a tall, older man wearing khakis and a long-sleeved shirt that was casually rolled up to the elbows greeted us in the waiting area. "Hello, I'm Mr. Walker. Call me Ed. Please come this way," he instructed.

The three of us followed Ed into a conference room where we were once again shown papers with dollar signs scattered across them. Robert and I looked at the numbers. *That's too much money. How are we going to pay that?* I wondered as Robert looked intently at the list.

"Would you like me to show you some lots?" Ed asked.

Why would I want to see a lot in a cemetery? I thought angrily.

Robert and I climbed into the back seat of Susan's car so Ed could sit in front next to her as she drove. "There's only one lot left for a standing stone. Do you want to see it?" Ed asked us. Robert and I both nodded. In response, Ed directed Susan to a lot along a narrow road lined with old tombstones and shade-giving trees.

As we stepped out of the car, I saw a wire fence separating the cemetery from an adjacent street. Listening to the swishing sounds of cars zooming by just beyond the fence, I sensed Andreas wouldn't get much rest here. "No, I don't like this place. It's too noisy," I told Ed.

"Could you show us some other lots?" Susan asked in her friendly manner.

"The others will require flat stones. Would you like a lot on the hill over there?"

I looked at the treeless, wide-open hill and couldn't imagine Andreas there either. He would be lonely. "No, it's too barren," I answered.

Susan continued driving, slowly guiding the car down a narrow path and stopping next to a short walkway lined by katsura trees with rustling, heart-shaped leaves. The walkway led us to a small piece of land available for a flat stone. Two ancient pines stood nearby. Their calm, grounded presence filled me with a sense of safety, like elders watching over my dear son. I immediately knew Andreas would like this place. Robert and Susan felt the same. "This is a gravesite for two or four . . . deep, extra deep, for two on two or cremation," Ed explained.

His words yanked my heart into a new reality. *I want to go home! I want to be there when Andreas returns. Who am I now?* I silently screamed. *Am I not who I was just two days ago? Now I'm being asked to do the unthinkable, the unimaginable: bury my son, my present, my future!*

When we returned to our house, friends, neighbors, and colleagues were already waiting for us. They had filled our dining room table with trays of food, including a large baked turkey, its familiar aroma reaching every corner of our home. Visitors had placed spiritual remembrance cards and booklets, some wrapped in silklike paper, on a side table. Each one was a special spiritual gift to let our family know that Andreas's name would be included in prayers for some time to come, prayers to help Andreas's soul rest in peace. *Will Andreas hear their prayers? Will he know that so many people love him and are outraged by what happened to him?*

Despite having visitors, I could not enjoy their company as I would have two days earlier. Though the outpouring of love and support helped our family get through those first days without Andreas, I felt ungrounded. With my reality shifting from present to past and back again, it was impossible to remain standing for long. The floor once again yanked me down. As our guests continued to speak in hushed tones, my eyes landed on Andreas's slightly ajar bedroom door. *Surely Andreas will get up soon. He hasn't had breakfast, and it's almost time for lunch. That's strange. He's an early riser like his dad, so he should be up by now, especially with all our guests here.*

I had often waited for Andreas to return home from school or playing sports or a friend's house. Now I stared at the door, longing for him to walk through it once more. But my weakened body laid out upon the carpet reminded me that what was normal just two days prior would never be again.

The next day, Tuesday, June 13, my brother Jürgen and his wife, Marlene, arrived from Caracas, Venezuela, as did Robert's mother from New Jersey. That warm evening, Robert, Tom, and I walked out of our house in silence as my brother, his wife, and my mother-in-law accompanied us to the funeral home to see Andreas. We drove up the street, parked our car, and walked toward the building's entrance where two staff members stood like sentries on guard at each side of the open doorway. Upon entering, I noticed huge flower arrangements of white roses, lilies, and carnations surrounding a large metal casket, and I immediately felt the floor underneath me begin to shake. I took a few steps toward the coffin where Andreas lay with his eyes closed. His eyebrows looked fuller and darker than they had just three days earlier. *That's not Andreas!* I silently screamed.

Andreas didn't move inside the box. He didn't acknowledge my presence. *That's not Andreas! Andreas will come home soon. It can't be him! Why would there be flowers surrounding Andreas instead of a stereo or CDs or tapes?* His wispy dark hair looked as if it had been re-created on a wax figure. *That's not Andreas!*

Seeing my son in the sage-green satin-lined casket propelled me toward the open door. I had to turn my back on him. While everyone else stayed near the coffin, I—Andreas's mother, the one who gave birth to him—could not bring myself to touch his motionless body.

—꿈—

Late that evening, after we returned home from the funeral parlor, my younger brother, Bernhard, and his son, Leonard, arrived from Houston.

Shortly before nine the next morning, two black limousines sent by the funeral home pulled up in front of our house. The conservatively dressed drivers helped us into the bellies of the cavernous vehicles. Each car had two long bench seats arranged horizontally so that passengers sat facing one another. I had never ridden in a car with doors that opened in the middle of the vehicle, and I never expected to be riding in one to bury my teenage son.

After a short drive, the limousines stopped in front of the stone chapel near the entrance to the cemetery, and the drivers opened the doors for us. Trapped in a nightmare, I couldn't sense my feet touching the ground as they moved to go inside. As Robert, Tom, and I walked down the aisle with the rest of our family, I was startled to see how crowded the chapel was. Everywhere I looked, I saw familiar people: Andreas's and Tom's friends, old friends of mine from college that I hadn't seen in years, family friends, coworkers, and past and present neighbors.

In front of the altar stood a coffin covered with a soft, white blanket. A large bouquet of red roses was placed next to a photo of Andreas. In it, he's sitting relaxed in a small motorboat on vacation in Maine with a perfect blue sky and the rippling white waves of the Atlantic behind him. With his wavy dark hair blown onto his brow, he holds a half-eaten vanilla cookie between his thumb and forefinger, and his young lips open a bit to convey a smile.

Some of those in attendance stood near the coffin in silence. Others made the sign of the cross and stepped toward the side of the chapel. Many waited in line to express their condolences to me and my family. But after the third person approached us, I could no longer stand there. *How does a mother stand still knowing her precious boy—the son she gave all her love to from the moment he was born—will forever disappear into the earth in a few minutes?* Like a lost and confused dog, I began wandering around the chapel, wanting to greet friends and chat with them about normal things. But all I could do was look at them in disbelief and stumble on. Even when I saw my college friends Barbara and Nancy, I couldn't find words. Our eyes locked, but we remained silent, so I moved on.

When I heard music coming from the back of the chapel, it startled me. "I'm gonna free-fall out into nothin' / Gonna leave this world for a while," sang Tom Petty. I turned to see Todd, Mike, and some of Andreas's other friends standing together, crying as the music played from a tape deck one of them had brought to the church. I'd heard this same melody just days earlier, through the closed door of Andreas's bedroom as he and Todd hung out together Saturday afternoon, laughing and listening to music before heading out that evening to the carnival. None of us could've known then that just hours later, Andreas would be fighting for his life in the local hospital.

Soon it was time to leave the chapel and climb back into the black cars. Robert, Tom, my mother-in-law, and I sat frozen to the seats in absolute silence as our limo pulled slowly away from the curb. The rest of our family followed. Many loved ones drove behind us as the funeral procession made its way past large tombstones and came to a stop at the narrow path that led to the grave site Robert and I had chosen two days earlier.

One of the men from the funeral home opened the door of our car, but upon seeing the brushed metal coffin among the gravestones, a powerful but unseen force pushed against my body and kept me seated. Somehow—I honestly can't remember how—I finally made my way to the graveside and took a seat on a plastic folding chair between Robert and Tom. I found myself staring at the coffin, which was adorned with red roses. It rested next to a hole in the ground and a heap of dirt covered by a blanket of bright green Astroturf. When the Reverend Charles Foreman from King's Chapel in Boston began to speak, I went numb.

"Bad things happen when people misuse their freedom and opt for violence," the reverend started. "We live in a violent society. To the young people here this afternoon, I want to say this: Violence is not the way to go. It is not the answer to any intelligent question at all. If you want to give meaning to Andreas's life and death, dedicate your wonderful strength and energy and gifts to building a community without violence, one with safe streets, safe neighborhoods, and safe schools. My generation has failed to find answers and solutions to violence, but your generation can and *must* do better. Be indignant and be angry at what has happened to Andreas. It's a bad thing. God does not will such madness. God calls us to life and wants wholeness for us. Our love for Andreas and his love for us—his friends and family—cannot be altered by time or circumstance. In the mysterious ways of love, be certain that Andreas will be with us in the months and years to come. Stay close to one another. If not today, may you yet discover the presence of God in your lives."

Safety has always been important to me. Toward the tail-end of World War II, with my father away serving in the German Army, my mother had to flee alone with my three-year-old brother, Jürgen, from her home in Crossen an der Oder, a small city on the banks of the Oder River in what was then eastern Germany but is now part of Poland. It was January 1945, and she was four months pregnant with me. While *auf der Flucht*, or on the run, my mother and Jürgen felt the constant fear of death as they experienced bombings, frigid temperatures, hunger, and homelessness.

During a long train ride from Berlin, my mother and brother sat between cars of injured soldiers. At one point, the train spent several days stopped in a tunnel to wait out air strikes. Eventually arriving in Garmisch-Partenkirchen, a town nestled in the Bavarian Alps in the southern part of Germany, my pregnant mother and brother were taken in as *Vertriebene,* or displaced people. It was there that I was born in June of 1945. The war had come to an end just weeks earlier, but my mother had no way of knowing if we'd ever see my father again. And then, by miracle or good fortune, my father did find us. Although we were refugees, our family of four was together at last.

During the early winter months of 1951, my father left Germany and took a boat from Genoa, Italy, to Venezuela to look for work. He had seen an advertisement in a German magazine from the Venezuelan government announcing that it was looking for technically trained and competent workers. At the time, I was five, Jürgen was nine, and our younger brother, Bernhard, who was also born in Garmisch-Partenkirchen, was four. Besides needing work, my father yearned to escape the memories of the war that had taken the lives of his parents and brother and left his sister forever changed.

A year and a half later, in October 1952, my mother, my two brothers, and I joined him in Venezuela. From Genoa, we took the Italian ship *Urania II,* which transported World War II refugees and immigrants to Venezuela. Shortly after our arrival in the tropical city of Maracaibo, and perhaps because I spoke not a word of Spanish, I was placed into the first grade even though back in Germany, I'd just started second grade. My new classmates neither looked nor spoke like me. I was fair-skinned with short, light brown hair like most girls I knew in Germany, whereas my new classmates had darker skin and most of them had curly, black hair. During the first few years after our arrival, we lived in a one-room, garage-like dwelling surrounded by other recently arrived refugees and immigrants from Europe who made their homes in similar structures near us.

In Maracaibo, with its palm trees, heat, and humidity, our family routine changed. We could no longer take Sunday walks through the cool forest or sit in the meadows and look up at the snowcapped Alps as we'd done in Germany. Instead, I saw little of my father except on weekends. He worked long hours in the boiler room of the local Catholic hospital to support our family, and my mother helped by washing sheets at home for the Hotel Bustamante, a local establishment owned by a German immigrant who had settled in Maracaibo years earlier. Every day after school, Jürgen, Bernhard, and I would help Mother fold the stiff, sun-dried cotton sheets, each of us holding one corner and pulling tightly to help straighten the sheets so it would be easier for her to iron them. Father would return from work on his motorcycle in the early evening. Then he'd pack the clean sheets, which were neatly folded and ironed, into the box on the back of his motorcycle, and drop them off at the hotel. Shortly afterward, he'd return with more soiled sheets to be washed the next day.

In 1956, after sharing a house with another refugee family for a few years, my parents' hard work paid off when they were able to rent a small house just for us and one housemate. While we were living at this house, my father began reading the local newspaper, *El Panorama*, on Sundays. I liked sitting next to him as he read. He would give me the paper-doll section, and I would cut out the dolls and match them to their dresses. Over time, as my father held up the paper to read, I began noticing photos of men and women who had been killed in our city. Those images on the back page of the newspaper became a constant reminder of potential dangers all around us. I vowed then and there that when I grew up and had children, they would feel and be safe. As part of the first generation of our family who didn't experience war firsthand—unless you count my experience in utero—I'd always hoped that my children would never know such conflict and violence. It never occurred to me that they could be the victims of an urban assault during peacetime.

—◊—

Robert, Andreas's father, was born in Berlin in October of 1940, during the initial bombing of the city by the British Air Force. When Robert was just two years old, his father, who had been away serving in the German Army, was able to arrange to have his wife and son evacuated from the war-torn city. The two went to live on a farm in the small village of Walddorf, Germany, which became Gdansk, Poland, after the war.

After the war ended in 1945, Robert and his mother returned to their war-ravaged city, living with Robert's paternal grandparents in their heavily damaged former apartment in what soon became the French sector of West Berlin. Robert grew up there, playing in bombed-out houses and buildings. When Robert was nine, his father returned to Germany after spending several years in Russia as a prisoner of war.

At age thirteen, Robert immigrated with his parents to the United States. Sponsored by his maternal aunt and uncle, who lived in Somerville, New Jersey, the family soon found a home in nearby North Plainfield, and Robert's father secured work as a toolmaker.

More than a decade later, in March of 1966, I arrived in Boston from Maracaibo to attend a six-month program at the Hickox Secretarial School on Boylston Street near the Public Garden and Boston Common. My goal was to improve my English and hone my office skills in hopes of getting a better paying and more interesting job upon my return to Venezuela.

By this time, Robert had already earned a bachelor's degree from Rutgers and a master's from the University of Pennsylvania and was pursuing a PhD in engineering from Penn. In 1966, when we met at an international student dance, he was living in Cambridge, taking specialized courses at Harvard, and working on his thesis. We immediately discovered that we both had parents from Germany, and more specifically, my father and his parents were from Berlin. That, and the fact that we were both immigrants, immediately bonded us.

After a few months in Boston, I returned to Maracaibo, where I was able to put my recently improved secretarial skills to work at a new job with an oil company. Although I enjoyed the work, the position was short-lived because it wasn't long before Robert and I decided to get married.

On August 10, 1967, in the presence of close family and friends, a justice of the peace married us at my parents' house in Maracaibo. Two days later, we celebrated our union in a second ceremony with a German pastor officiating at a Lutheran church. Afterward, we held a small gathering at a nearby club.

A few months later, after I'd received the documents needed to immigrate to the United States, I joined Robert in Cambridge, Massachusetts, where our son Thomas was born in June of 1968. When our one-bedroom apartment became too small for our expanding family, we moved to the two-family house in Belmont.

When we first stepped into the house in the fall of 1969, just four months before Andreas was born, it immediately felt like home. It was in a neighborhood with young families and children all around, and we particularly liked that the house was next to a playground with a big maple tree, a sandbox, swings, a slide, and an expansive grass field behind it. I imagined Thomas and his little brother or sister running across the field. And as I watched mothers catch their children at the end of the slide, I couldn't wait to take Tom and the baby I was carrying and do the same.

Waking up on the floor the morning after the funeral, I forced myself to stand up to greet my brothers, my sister-in-law, and my nephew, who were staying with my neighbors. It was my forty-fourth birthday, and they'd come to share breakfast with me. Robert encouraged me to sit at our dining room table, but it took all my energy just to remain upright in the chair. I looked at the slice of toast on the plate in front of me, but I couldn't make my hands move to pick it up. My family sat at the table, waiting for me to eat.

Standing next to me, Robert looked around the table as he put his hand on my shoulder. Then, in unison, he and my brothers said hesitatingly, "Happy Birthday."

"*Birthday!*" I screamed. "How can I have a birthday when Andreas is lying dead under a heap of dirt? How can I?" Everybody around the table winced as my hands—my useless hands that couldn't touch or comfort my son—remained on my lap.

Who's having a birthday? Did I not die with Andreas? I longed for Andreas to open our back door, walk up the stairs, and say, "Mom, I'm home! I'm back!"

That afternoon, the sun shined brightly as Robert and I drove to Boston's Logan Airport. My parents, who were seldom able to visit us, were now returning to the States from Germany, a day after Andreas's burial and only a month after being here in May to spend Mother's Day with our family of four. The pictures we took of all of us smiling in front of our blooming dogwood tree were still undeveloped in our camera. My parents had no idea when they'd left then that they would never see Andreas again. As it turned out, they couldn't even attend his funeral, which took place just three days after his death. Making travel arrangements for the transatlantic trip from their tiny village took time.

I could still hear my voice shaking as I recalled phoning them in Germany with the news that Andreas had been murdered. "Sie haben Andreas ermordet! Sie haben Andreas ermordet!" I kept repeating to my father, tears drenching my blouse.

The news instantly reopened wounds from my father's own traumatic experiences during the war. His voice hurt my ears as he screamed into the phone, "Ich dachte der Krieg ist vorbei!" ("I thought the war was over!") The next thing I heard was a crashing sound as the phone fell from his hand to the floor. Moments later, my mother picked up the receiver and said in a trembling voice, "Ach du mein Kind!" ("Oh my dear child!")

Robert and I walked in silence toward the international arrival gate and stood among the joyful men and women gathered around waiting for their loved ones. Normally, I would crane my neck excitedly, trying to catch a glimpse of my parents as they meandered their way through the labyrinth of immigration and customs. But not this time. Instead, I wondered, *Will they comfort me and take away my pain? Will they put their arms around my hurting body? How will they look?*

Suddenly, the door flung open, letting a stream of travelers flow into the lobby. Through the opened door, I saw an older man and woman at the end of the long line of people still inside the customs room. *Is that Mutti and Vati?* When the door opened a few minutes later, I saw my mom and dad in the distance. *Is it really them?* Robert and I did not lift our arms to wave; we just set our bodies in motion and walked toward the open door.

With his body hunched forward, my father shuffled toward us, looking much older than he had just a month before. He didn't greet us with a smile as he usually did. Instead, he glanced at me with his chestnut-brown eyes, then looked down at the floor. His face appeared disjointed, like a Picasso painting, as if his features had shifted from the force of the news of his grandson's murder. He did not reach out to embrace me.

My mother walked next to him. Her slender body looked contorted, as if something had crushed her strong bones—the same bones that, on previous visits, had allowed her to stand up straight and run over to hug her grandsons. Now her arms hung limply at her sides.

Robert and I looked at my parents without saying a word. Robert reached out and grabbed their small suitcase, then the four of us walked in silence through the airport toward the parking garage, our collective pain so deep there were no words.

CHAPTER 2

Investigation

One thing I learned early on after Andreas's murder was that my family would not be left alone to grieve. A few days after Andreas was killed, the assistant district attorney summoned us to the courthouse to meet with him. On the morning of June 16, the day after my parents arrived, we were expecting the victim advocate assigned to our case by the Cambridge Superior Court to accompany us to the meeting. Close to the time she had told Robert we could anticipate her arrival, I looked out our second-floor living room window and saw that there was a young woman waiting below on the front walkway. I didn't know what kind of person to envisage on that bright summer morning just five days after Andreas was murdered. I'd never seen a victim advocate before. Slender and elegant in her beige two-piece dress suit and mauve scarf, the sun glinted off her short black hair. *I don't want to meet this woman. Go away! I want my life back,* I thought to myself.

Dressed in the blue, floral-print skirt and white blouse I'd worn to my job as a special education social worker on my last day at work before Andreas was killed, I went to tell Robert that our victim advocate had arrived. "Are you ready?" I asked through our slightly ajar bedroom door.

The sound of footsteps answered me, but soon, Robert stepped out of the room looking as if he were lost in his own home, going back and forth between the bathroom and bedroom a few times. Clad in gray pants and a white T-shirt, he stood still for a moment and stared at a collection of button-down dress shirts that he'd placed on the bed.

How does one dress for a visit with the attorney prosecuting the murder of one's son? I wondered.

Robert put on a light blue shirt and picked up a tie from the hanger on the closet door. Then he hurried back to the bathroom and looked in the mirror; his oval face was as white as a sheet of paper.

"I'm almost done," Tom said from behind his closed bedroom door.

It was difficult for me to pass by Andreas's empty room the way I used to just a few days earlier when life was about enjoying the summer. Robert and I had happily anticipated both boys being home from college on summer break. Tom and Andreas had already started their summer jobs and were looking forward to spending time with friends.

As I descended our front stairs behind Robert and Tom, the hammering of my heart grew louder. Each step was bringing me closer to a person I never wanted to meet. Barely able to control my shaking hands, I locked the front door behind us.

I don't want to meet her! I don't! Go away! Just let me have Andreas back!

I wanted to turn around, go back into the kitchen, and make pancakes for Andreas, but my feet, as if disconnected from the rest of my body, walked slowly toward the victim advocate.

"Good morning," she said in a gentle tone as she reached her right hand toward Robert. "Nice to meet you. I'm Lucy Murray-Brown. I believe we've spoken on the phone."

Robert returned her handshake, but his face was unchanged from when he looked in the bathroom mirror.

"I'm so sorry about what happened to Andreas," Lucy added.

I stood silently beside Robert. *I don't want to meet her! I don't!* As the voice inside my head kept screaming, *I don't want to meet her,* I sensed my right arm reach toward Lucy to shake her delicate hand. "Hi, I'm Christine. I'm glad to meet you too," I heard myself say. Touched by the compassion reflected in the warmth of her eyes, tears flowed down my cheeks.

Tom stood just a few feet away, his cocoa-colored eyes twitching; these were the same eyes that just six days earlier had twinkled with youthful exuberance in anticipation of spending the summer with his younger brother. Having taken a year off after high school, Tom had just completed his freshman year at the University of Maine in Orono. With Andreas at UMass Lowell, the past school year was only the second time they'd ever been apart for more than a short period, and their recent reunion had been a happy one filled with brotherly jokes and laughter.

Now, standing outside our home meeting our victim advocate, Tom's youthful lightness had disappeared. He looked like a different person, one totally taken over by the harsh horror of losing his brother to violence. In that moment, I realized I no longer knew how to reach out to him. Seeing the pain of Andreas's violent death reflected in each other created an immense chasm between us. We could no longer connect in the way we had before.

What if Andreas comes home while we're gone? I worried as Tom and I sat silently in the back seat of Lucy's car. *How strange to see Robert sitting in front next to Lucy instead of driving our car. Our lives are over!*

As Tom sat next to me in his own darkness, I gazed out the window of the moving car. Even though it was a sunny morning, fog covered our neighborhood, giving the houses a surreal appearance.

Could it be that Andreas had anything to do with what happened to him? No, it can't be. He was such a thoughtful son, our peacekeeper. It's impossible to think, but maybe I didn't really know him anymore. Did he have another life? It can't be!

After Lucy parked on a side street near the courthouse, we uncoiled our bodies, climbed out of the car, and, for a moment, stood like statues on the sidewalk. Then we slowly turned and walked toward the imposing concrete building in the distance, following Lucy into an unknown world. I had a hard time keeping up with the three of them because my body was reluctant to move forward. The pounding of my heart intensified as we approached the entrance to the courthouse.

What's the prosecutor going to tell us? All I want to hear is that the one who did this is locked up. I also want to know why he killed Andreas. Will he tell us that? I don't want to go into this building and meet the prosecutor. Will he blame me for not having taken care of Andreas as a mother should? I want to go home so I can be there when Andreas gets up!

"At the entrance, some guards will search our bags," Lucy informed us before entering the building.

Sure enough, once we passed the main door, two security guards asked me to place my handbag on a moving belt. *These scanners and metal detectors are just like at the airport. Where am I? What am I doing here?*

After she made it through security, Lucy waited for us. When we finally stepped into the belly of the building, I looked around and was struck by the beauty of the grand marble staircase in front of us. For a moment, I stood mesmerized by its graceful, serpentine form.

"We're going to take the elevator over there to the fourth floor," Lucy said as she motioned for us to follow her across the busy lobby.

What are all these people doing here? Am I at the airport going on a trip? Men and women, most of them in dark business suits, rushed across the lobby. Some sat next to more casually dressed, frightened-looking young men and women on wooden benches. Others, as if confused about their destination, just took a few steps, stopped, and then moved on. This shattered my illusion of being at the airport. Their grave looks gave me the impression that they were dealing with urgent matters. *What are they all doing here? What's the prosecutor going to tell us? Will he ask us questions about Andreas? Will he tell us that it was Andreas's fault?*

After being locked in the slow-moving elevator for what seemed like a long time, we arrived on the fourth floor. We followed Lucy through a web of corridors and rooms until she stopped at an open door. "This is Mr. Rapacki's office. Please wait while I find him and let him know we're here."

As I scanned the large room, Robert and Tom stood frozen, staring straight ahead. Boxes holding overstuffed accordion folders, their cords stretched to accommodate the bulging contents, sat on the floor lining the perimeter of the room. Dozens of manila folders, labeled and color coded, were piled in high, uneven stacks on the gray metal desk. My eyes skipped from box to box and over the desk, confused by the disorder but alert for any movement indicating the appearance of the prosecutor.

After a few minutes, Lucy reappeared at the open office door. "Please have a seat," she said, pointing us to a few casually arranged plastic chairs by the desk. Her upper body twisted slightly as she looked over her shoulder and nodded at the man standing behind her. "Meet Mr. Rapacki."

I was stunned when I saw a noticeably young man with wavy, blond hair standing in the doorway. *This is Mr. Rapacki? He has a baby face! He can't be much older than Tom or Andreas! How is he going to be able to convict the murderer?*

Mr. Rapacki gave the three of us a quick glance with his sapphire eyes as he walked into the room toward his seat behind the desk. "Nice to meet you," he said, still standing and leaning slightly across the cluttered surface to shake Robert's hand. "Please take a seat." His firm voice, penetrating eyes, and somber face instantly reminded me of the border police I'd encountered as a teenager while visiting my grandmother in Finsterwalde.

Once, aboard the *Interzonenzug* (interzone) train from Frankfurt, I pushed open a window when we stopped at Gerstungen, a border station in communist East Germany. I was curious where we were and eager to get some fresh air. "Zurück bleiben! Fenster schliessen!" ("Stay back! Close the window!") the guards shouted from the train platform. Their voices propelled me back to my seat among older men and women dressed in black. My face turned crimson, and my heart raced out of control.

The doors creaked as the guards entered the train. I knew they were nearing my section when I heard the excited sniffing and panting of their German shepherds. As the guards flung open the door, every man and woman in my compartment tensed and silenced their previously friendly conversations. We all gazed vacantly as if trying to make ourselves invisible.

A guard in a grayish-green military uniform with two guns attached to his belt with black holsters burst into the compartment and shouted, "Pass Kontrolle!" ("Passport control!") When he took my passport, he eyed the front cover, turned it around, looked at the back, and again stared at the front as if he'd never seen one from Venezuela before. He opened it slowly while glaring at me, then fixed his gaze on my photo, lifted his head, and questioned, "Why are you coming to East Germany?"

"I'm going to visit my grandmother and uncle in Finsterwalde," I replied in a soft voice, afraid that my answer wasn't what he wanted to hear.

He pulled out a pink index card, one that I'd sent to the authorities well in advance of my trip, requesting permission to enter East Germany. While he scrutinized the card in his hand as if comparing my spoken words to what I had written down, my fellow travelers sunk deeper into their seats. We all breathed a sigh of relief after the guard turned around and left the compartment. We remained silent for a very long time after that.

But now, for the sake of my slain child, I had to sit on the rigid plastic chair in front of the prosecutor's desk alongside my husband and remaining son. Mr. Rapacki's eyes narrowed as he looked at us over his cluttered desk and spoke plainly. "My job as the assistant district attorney is to charge and then prosecute someone for the murder of your son," he said. Then he took a quick breath and added, "It hasn't been easy to get information."

Hearing the words *murder* and *your son* next to each other, and spoken so directly, shattered my heart and made it difficult for me to focus on what was being said. As I tried to pull my attention back to the conversation, I could feel my body tighten, much like it had on that train decades earlier. I sensed Tom's body stiffen next to mine. Robert's usual deep voice turned softer, hesitant, as he sought answers from Mr. Rapacki about what had happened in the final moments of Andreas's life.

While the prosecutor responded to each of Robert's questions, my ears ceased to work as I thought only of the words I longed to hear Mr. Rapacki say: "This has all been a big mistake, a cruel joke. Andreas is here, and he's ready to go home with you." Yet those words never flowed from the prosecutor's mouth; they only repeated themselves in my mind. But soon the weight of Mr. Rapacki's actual words and the graphic images they painted cut through my thoughts and made my body weak. In an effort to keep myself upright, I curled my hands around the armrest of the chair for support.

Wake up! Wake up! I begged myself, trying to stop the nightmare. But no matter how hard I tried to wake up, no other reality materialized. Traumatized, it seemed I could both hear and see Mr. Rapacki's words as they tumbled across the desktop toward us in slow motion; each one adding to the unbearable mental picture of what had happened to Andreas. As the prosecutor continued to speak, my gaze moved to the boxes lined up along the office wall. *These boxes are filled with evidence. Is Andreas's green-striped shirt—the one he carefully ironed and wore when he went out last Saturday night—in one of these boxes? I really don't want to know.*

Images of Andreas's bloodstained sneakers suspended on my outstretched hands flashed through my mind. Todd and Mike, the friends who were with him during the attack, brought them to me Saturday night when they came to tell me that Andreas had been hurt. I kept hearing more words that I could barely comprehend when, suddenly, Mr. Rapacki squinted and stared straight at me. *What now?* I thought, perplexed.

"I bet you don't know what your son was wearing that night," he stated as if fact. Confused, his words made no sense to me as they slithered across the desk and wormed their way into my mind. Pausing for emphasis, he added, "Did you know your son and his friends were drinking?" His words felt accusatory and hit the most vulnerable spot in my heart, silencing any possible response.

A sense of foreboding overcame me as my thoughts turned into tangled sensations. I couldn't formulate an answer for Mr. Rapacki; I could only shake my head from side to side. *Am I the guilty one?* I wondered. *Did I do something wrong? Andreas was such a considerate young man. Did I not raise him well? If I'd done a better job as a mother, would he still be alive?*

Interrupting my anxious and fearful thoughts, Robert asked, "Has anybody been arrested yet?"

"NO!" Mr. Rapacki emphatically replied. Seeming almost surprised at the abrasiveness of his own voice, he took a breath and continued in a calmer tone. "It's been very difficult for the police to track down a suspect," he said. "The knife that was used broke in two during the stabbing, and the handle was found in a pool of blood, so we haven't been able to get fingerprints off it." The prosecutor's words slammed into my body, flooding my mind with bloody images.

That's Andreas's blood he's referring to. How much force did the murderer use to stab him? How much did Andreas suffer? How much? How much? The murderer hasn't been caught? How can that be? Let me out of here! I can't take this anymore! As the room began to spin, I stood up and stumbled to the door. Lucy followed me.

Senseless killing! I could scream and never stop. Where are you, Andreas?

—⟋⟋⟋—

The following week, we received a call from Lucy who had been regularly communicating with us in the aftermath of Andreas's death. Though her calls were well intentioned and meant to provide us with information and helpful support as we navigated the criminal justice system, they could feel excruciatingly painful and disorienting amidst our intense grief. Still, hers was a voice of caring. Lucy acted much like a spiritual guide, holding us steady as she provided vital information with clarity and compassion. We understood that it was imperative for us to be well informed about what the prosecutor's office was doing to find our son's murderer and bring him to justice. I was grateful and relieved that Robert was willing to take these calls. The time or two I had found myself on the other end of the line with Lucy—even though her voice was soothing and I appreciated her helpfulness—I had difficulty concentrating on her words and comprehending what she was telling me. Robert, who was naturally more grounded and analytical, was able to absorb the information Lucy provided and ask the important questions that needed asking. Now, standing next to Robert by the phone in the kitchen, I noticed his brow was deeply furrowed.

"What's the matter?" I asked after he hung up, knowing I should inquire but not really wanting to know.

"The police arrested the person they think killed Andreas. He was arraigned today."

"Does that mean he's in jail?" I questioned.

"He's being held for now. He must appear before the grand jury."

"What's a grand jury?" All of this was unfamiliar to me.

"They'll decide whether there's enough evidence to charge him with the crime," Robert explained.

"Will he stay in jail?"

"His lawyer is trying to get him out on bail," Robert calmly continued.

"Out on bail! Does that mean he'll be free again?" I exclaimed, wanting to hear a resolute no.

Robert answered softly, "Yes. If he makes bail, he'll be back on the streets."

"Back on the streets?" I shouted, echoing Robert's reply. "How can someone accused of killing another person be allowed back on the streets?"

Robert went to the living room to watch TV. I turned around toward the sink. *Andreas is coming home soon. I'll clean the dishes and start preparing dinner. He can help me cut up the onions. He does it much faster than I do, and, besides, he can cut them without his eyes watering. Andreas, will you help me cook dinner tonight?* I asked in my mind, knowing very well that he wouldn't answer.

The following day, I visited Andreas at Mount Auburn Cemetery in Cambridge. It was a brilliant summer afternoon as I stood at his grave and looked up at the immense blue sky above me with not a single cloud in sight. The leaves on the katsura trees near Andreas's burial site had turned from a lighter shamrock green to a deep emerald. Feathery grass filaments were beginning to appear through the damp earth that had become Andreas's unliftable blanket. *God, please let me see the wispy, adolescent fuzz upon his chin. Please, just one more time.*

When I returned home, it seemed strange to find mail and a folded newspaper in the box out front. It was proof that life goes on, but I had no intention of reading any of it because I could no longer absorb new information. Nothing I read made sense anymore.

I threw the mail and paper onto our dining room table the way I'd always done. Suddenly, as if the newspaper had a life of its own, it unfolded, exposing the front-page headline: "Murder Suspect Arrested." The corresponding photo of a young white man caused my body to lurch as if I'd been hit with a jolt of electricity. Gasping for air, I began pacing alongside the table, back and forth, back and forth, while trying to extricate my eyes from what I'd just seen. Even when I looked away, I couldn't erase the image forming in my mind of the young man in the newspaper holding a huge kitchen knife in his hand. *He's haunting me!* I screamed internally, still pacing around our dining room. With all my strength, I propelled my body into the kitchen, trying in vain to escape, but fear and the image of that young man followed me. *That devil's face is in my home! I don't want his image in my mind!* I stood frozen in the kitchen. He'd invaded my broken home to destroy what remained of my life spirit, just as he had destroyed Andreas's life. *Is there no end to it?* I wailed silently.

I returned to the dining room and saw the cold look of that young man staring back at me from Andreas's empty place at the table. *Is he talking to me? Is he taunting me by saying, "I'm here. I'm still alive!"*

My body trembled as I realized that sometime soon, I'd face this young man. I also knew that Andreas would never again sit at this table, never again eat another meal with us, never again make us laugh. *Andreas, when are you coming back? I'm waiting for you.*

Sometime later, Lucy again spoke to Robert on the phone. His face turned to stone as he said grimly, "He's out on bail."

"So the rumors I've heard of him playing basketball near his house are true?" I asked incredulously. I felt a heavy thumping in my chest, knowing that Andreas would never again smile at his teammates, Tim and Mike, when they applauded him for a good move he made in a game of basketball. I stayed in the kitchen with tears streaming down my face as Robert turned around and walked back into the living room without saying a word.

*How is it possible that the one accused of murdering Andreas can
still play under the sunny summer sky, while Andreas lies buried under
a pile of dirt?*

*Now that he's out on bail, will the accused be working at the super-
market where we shop? What if he kills another of Andreas's friends?
Will he wait for me at Andreas's grave to kill me too?* In an attempt to
stay calm, I told myself, *Don't think that way. There's no choice but to
go on with your life.*

Fear began to permeate our home, and we stayed away from our
windows. Robert and Tom also became more watchful. I noticed
that they looked in all directions when they approached their cars in
our driveway. They frequently checked the doorknobs of our house
to make sure they were locked and secure. Robert even installed
heavier locks with chains. Still, I doubted, *Are they strong enough to
withstand an attack?*

When someone you love is alive one moment and violently ripped
out of your life the next, it makes you question your own mortality.
Since Andreas's death, time had taken on a new significance in my
life. At 11:24 a.m. on Saturday, July 1, recording the exact time I made
the journal entry, I wrote, "Love is the only consolation, but love did
not keep Andreas alive."

Later that day, I had a strong urge to step back into the world I knew
before Andreas was murdered. *Is there anything left of that life?* I pon-
dered. I decided that I'd go to the mall where Andreas used to shop
for his back-to-school clothes. It was only a few minutes away from
our house, and with many people there, it seemed like a safe place.

After staring at my car keys for a long time, I imagined getting
into my car, turning on the engine, and leaving the house by myself.
Three weeks had passed since Andreas was killed, and during that

time, I hadn't gone out alone other than to the cemetery. When I finally summoned the courage, I told Robert, who was sitting at his desk working, where I was going.

Clutching the steering wheel tightly, I drove slowly down the once familiar streets. After I arrived, I sat in the mall parking lot watching people come and go for a bit. Eventually, I opened the car door and twisted my body sideways to ease my legs out. Once my sandals touched the ground and I could feel that it was solid, I stood up. As if learning how to walk again on my own, I placed one foot in front of the other very carefully until I reached the mall's large glass door.

I'd been to this place many times before, but suddenly, it all seemed strange and foreign to me. *I've seen this door before, but something feels unfamiliar now.* When I noticed a group of mothers and their young children rushing out the exit door, I couldn't help but think, *Those women are letting their children run ahead of them without fear.*

Once inside, I saw a large group of noisy teenage boys coming from the opposite direction. As they moved closer, I had a surreal thought: *Are these boys the ones who attacked Andreas?* Even though I had seen a photo of the accused, I couldn't help but wonder as I stood there in shock, looking from one teen to the other, *Is he the one who killed Andreas? No, maybe it's him. Why are they coming toward me?* My heart beat out of control as the mall seemed to spin. *Someone is going to get me from behind. What if the boy walking next to me is the one? I need to get out of here now! Turn around and get out!* But I couldn't get my feet to speed up. *Stop following me!* I screamed silently.

Finally, after what seemed like an eternity, I reached my car. Before opening the door, I looked back to make sure none of the young men had followed me. Then I opened the car door, sat inside, and pushed down the lock. White-knuckled, I tightly grasped the steering wheel the whole way home.

How long will he be out on bail? How much longer must I fear being killed as well?

CHAPTER 3

Longing

A few days after my panic-stricken excursion to the mall, I picked up my friend Boa, and we drove about ninety miles west to visit a psychic in Amherst. Boa's son Olaf, who loved to play the electric guitar, was one of Andreas's closest childhood friends. In those early years, Olaf and Andreas spent much time drawing, even sketching a carefully detailed layout of how Andreas might turn our attic into a room for himself. Four weeks before Andreas was murdered, our family was shocked to learn that Olaf had died in a car accident. Speechless and in much pain, Robert, Thomas, Andreas, and I had stood by Boa at the cemetery.

Like me, Boa was still in shock and grieving. We were both stunned by the fact that our sons were physically gone. In the depths of our love and yearning, it was impossible to believe that they just ceased to exist. We set out to see the psychic in hopes of learning something that would ease our pain.

After a couple hours on the road, we parked in a driveway surrounded by towering pine trees. "Are you sure you still want to see the psychic?" I asked Boa, a part of me hoping she'd say that she'd rather take a walk instead.

But Boa was undeterred. She needed to talk to this psychic that friends had told her could communicate with departed loved ones. "I have to get in touch with Olaf. He can't just *not* exist anymore," Boa said with tears in her eyes.

"I'm scared that the psychic will contact Andreas, even though I'm still waiting for him to come home tonight and have dinner with us," I said as tears rolled down my cheeks.

"I feel like that too. I still can't believe Olaf is really gone, even though I know he is. But where *is* he? Does his spirit still exist? I have to know. I didn't get to say goodbye," Boa explained before stepping out of the car.

As we walked toward the small wooden house, I exclaimed, "This place is beautiful! Look at those pine trees, Boa. They're magnificent!" Wishing we could stay outside among the trees and rolling hills, I continued, "I'm really nervous. I'm not sure I want to talk to the psychic."

"I'm nervous too, so I'll go first. You can see how it goes for me before you decide whether you want to see her."

Boa stepped forward and rang the doorbell. After a moment, she gently turned the knob and walked through the front door since the psychic was expecting us. *What will I see? What will I hear?* I asked myself. *Is she merely a charlatan who preys on vulnerable people to make a living?*

As I followed Boa into the spacious living room, I took everything in, hyperalert, as if my body was covered with eyes. The home was bright but sparsely furnished, and the sweet, woodsy scent of incense welcomed us. Boa and I sat in cozy rocking chairs as we waited for the psychic. Seeing the expansive verdant hills through the picture window helped calm my fearful heart a bit. "I wish I could just sit here and stare out the window," I whispered to Boa. She cried softly and did not respond.

After a few minutes, a young woman in a flowing indigo-colored skirt and flowery blouse entered the room so gracefully that she appeared to be floating across the floor. With a calm presence and long, black hair that framed her luminous face, I immediately felt at ease.

"Hello, Boa and Christine. I'm Sofia. Which one of you would like to go first?"

"I will," Boa replied.

As Boa followed Sofia into another room, I tried to relax while waiting my turn. My heart raced, overwhelmed by a flood of mixed emotions and uncertain whether I should've come to see the psychic at all. Part of me wished Sofia wouldn't make contact with Andreas in another realm, so as not to shatter the illusion that he would still come home. With my heart pounding, I listened for any signs of movement. *When Boa comes out, will she give me a signal to let me know whether I should go in next? How will I know?*

Before long, the door opened and Boa emerged, her face looking moist and puffy. The young psychic walked beside her, just as serene as before. Boa nodded to me as she returned to her seat in the waiting room.

As I followed Sofia into a dimly lit room, my gaze was immediately drawn to the glistening stones illuminating her space. Twinkling glass beads of translucent green, orange, and blue lay on small tables. A few tall candles flickered in two corners, adding a warm glow to the room.

"Please sit down," Sofia motioned toward a round pillow on the floor next to the candles. My body felt heavy, and it was difficult for me to relax into the cushion, but like a feather, Sofia drifted down onto the pillow across from me. She looked into my teary eyes and began asking me questions. But I was so inundated by the enormity of my feelings that later on, I couldn't recall a single thing she'd asked me. And before I knew it, she stopped her queries and instead suggested, "Let's get up. I want you to lie down over here."

I pulled myself up from the floor and stepped toward a cot covered with a pink sheet. Sofia motioned for me to lie down with my head toward the candles. As I rested on the cot, she initially remained standing beside me. *Is she trying to make me feel comfortable?* I wondered. *Does she sense that my channels are blocked from the pain I'm feeling?*

After a few minutes, she began telling me a story. "I come from a very large family, but most of my relatives are dead now. I was particularly close to my grandmother. Luckily, I was able to be with her when she passed on. As she lingered between life and death, she traveled back and forth between this earthly plane and the other side, or what we refer to as death. One time, when she returned from the other side, she told me she'd seen her sisters, my great-aunts. They were all cheering her on to come and be with them. I've talked to my grandmother many times since she passed on, and I know she's happy now because the last time I communicated with her, she told me she's with her sisters. Since that experience, I'm no longer afraid of death because I know our souls never truly die."

She's so lucky to have been present when her grandmother died, I thought. *I didn't even get to say goodbye to Andreas. I couldn't hold him and watch him slip into the other realm.* As my tears wet the sheet where my head lay, a flicker of light struggled to come alive inside my aching heart while I listened to Sofia's story, but my soul kept crying out: *I want Andreas now, in the flesh. I don't care to join him when I die. I want him here now!* I tried to relax so the psychic could begin her work, but I couldn't shut off my fearful heart. *I want her to find Andreas on the other side, but what if all she finds is a void? If that happens, where is Andreas?*

After Sofia told her story, she stood at my feet. I tried to feel her calming presence, but no matter how hard I tried, all I sensed were waves crashing within me. The flicker of light and hope in my heart was snuffed out. I tried to concentrate on Sofia's position and actions by keeping my body very still as her hands hovered above my feet then just above my sides. After a little while, she moved to stand behind me and placed her hands close to the crown of my head.

Suddenly, I heard a gurgling sound. It was hard to decipher at first, but gradually, slowly, as if coming from a distant place, the sound became discernible as Sofia said, "I can't see Andreas clearly, but he wants you to look into a paper shopping bag in his bedroom closet. There are things in it that he wants you to see."

I don't want Andreas to talk through Sofia! I want him to speak to me—in person! Andreas is going to be home for dinner tonight in his body, not in spirit, I argued with myself internally. *But what if there is a shopping bag in his closet? Then it means Andreas really is dead—that he* does *exist in another realm. I want him home, not in this other realm!*

After my session with the psychic ended, Boa and I, faces puffy and tear-stained, silently returned to the car. After driving a few miles through the rural part of western Massachusetts, Boa began to moan and exclaimed between sobs, "Sofia told me Olaf is playing music. He's having a great time." Boa caught her breath, then continued to speak angrily, "I want him to have a fabulous time here with us! I'm glad he's not suffering, but why couldn't he have fun up there *after* he finishes growing up with us down here?"

At first, I couldn't put into words what Sofia had said to me. Just the thought of Andreas in spirit was too much to bear. Eventually, though, little by little during the two-hour drive back, I was able to allow a few words to escape. "She told me there's a bag in Andreas's closet that he wants me to see," I began, my throat tight. I sobbed as I continued, "I really didn't want to hear it. I don't think I can go into his room. It's still the same, . . . like he just stepped out and is coming right back."

Later that day, as the afternoon sun cast shadows on the walls, the thought of what the psychic had shared compelled me to go to Andreas's room, albeit hesitantly. I slowly walked through his open bedroom door and stood in the center of the room in silence. *This is his space,* I thought. *I don't want to snoop around in it. Andreas wouldn't like that. I'll just ask him about the bag in his closet when he gets home tonight.* But the closet door, which was slightly ajar, seemed to beckon to me like an invitation.

At that instant, I heard my son's voice in the form of a whisper deep inside me, "Mom, look at it." My heart pounded as my right hand, acting as if detached from my body, seemingly floated toward the doorknob. My fingers closed around it, and I pulled until the closet door was fully open, looking back to see if anyone was watching me. Andreas's bed was still covered with his royal-blue fleece blanket with the silvery-gray eagle design, just waiting for his return. His portable stereo stood on his desk next to a stack of tapes, CDs, and notebooks. Holding my breath, I turned back to the closet and reluctantly reached through his hanging pants and shirts until my hand sensed something other than clothing in a far corner. Startled, my fingers grazed the rough surface of a paper bag. I let my hand rest on it for a moment as I contemplated my next move. *Should I take it out or ignore it and forget the psychic's words?*

Overcome by curiosity, I tugged on the sack, carefully pulling it toward the front of the closet. *How strange,* I thought. *It's just a simple shopping bag. What's it doing in his closet? What's in it?* I slowly began to peel back each folded corner with my fingertips, like plucking rose petals off a bud. Inside the bag, my lavender skirt, a white cotton blouse, and other summer clothes sat folded together. *I can't believe it! I've been looking everywhere for these!*

As tears rolled down my face, I suddenly had a vague recollection of storing my summer things in the back of Andreas's neatly organized closet at the end of the previous summer. I pulled my favorite pink-striped blouse from the bag and held it close to my heart as if I were embracing Andreas. I recalled my session with Sofia and thought, *He's still with me.* Suddenly, just as the sun was setting outside the bedroom windows, a glimmer of light radiated through the darkness of my shattered heart.

—◆◆◆—

Not long after Boa and I visited the psychic, I went into the basement to do some laundry. *Andreas, your clean clothes are still lying on top of the dryer,* I silently said to my son. *I haven't seen you wear them;*

they're just sitting there folded up. You look so handsome in those jeans and colorful T-shirts. Why haven't you been wearing them?

Where are you, Andreas? I feel this oppressive stillness in our home. There are no more phone calls from your friends. I long to hear Mike and Todd ask, "Hi, Mrs. Dresp. Is Andreas there?" I also haven't heard from your friend Jack, although I saw him at the gas station where he works. The instant I spotted him at the cash register, my heart began to race. But when our eyes met, I rushed out of the store.

Andreas, today I put the last photos we took of you on the dining room hutch. You remember, the ones from Mother's Day when Oma and Opa were visiting from Germany? I placed the bouquet of yellow roses they left for you next to the pictures. I kept staring at your smiling face. Your eyes, the color of bittersweet chocolate and so much like mine, looked back at me as if you might come through the frame. Your lips were slightly parted as though you'd just said something funny and were waiting for me to react.

Andreas, please, please, please come through the glass picture frame! This frame can't hold your six-foot, two-inch body. Please come home! If I break the glass, will you return to me?

One evening in mid-July, more than a month since I'd last seen Andreas, the shrill ring of the telephone made my heart lurch. I hesitated to answer it because I just wanted to be left alone. I didn't want to listen to anybody telling me to get out of the house and move on. But, after several rings, I lifted the receiver as if it were a prickly cactus, guided it toward my ear, and said hello.

"Hi, Christine. It's Ros."

"Hi," I responded, glad to hear her familiar voice.

"Mary, Ruth, and I would love to see you. Could you join us for breakfast on Thursday?" Ros asked.

Noticing a quivering sensation deep inside me, my throat tightened up and I found myself unable to answer. Scrambled words could not push their way through my many thoughts and feelings. *How strange that they want to include me in their gathering,* I thought. *Don't I now belong to an utterly different world from theirs?* My entire world, including my life as a social worker in the school system, had abruptly ended the day Andreas was killed.

As Ros continued to talk in her friendly manner, my anxiety began to subside. When she finished speaking, I was silent for what seemed like a long time before finally responding, "I need to think about it." *What would I do in their midst?* I wondered. *Aren't I forever broken? Is it possible to bridge the chasm ripped open between us by a young man with a knife?* The thought of sitting down to a meal just to chat with my coworkers, like we used to do occasionally over dinner, seemed so strange. It was as if Ros was a ghost from a long ago past whose sounds and images had faded. Despite the chasm, I felt the warmth in her voice. Her words drew me in, reminding me that parts of my former life were still out there somewhere, even if they felt lost to me now.

"We're planning to meet at this nice restaurant at a hotel in the woods," Ros said, practically begging me to join them.

Someone might attack me in the parking lot of the hotel, I worried. Finally, I said to Ros, "I'd love to see you all, but I don't know if I can make myself get out of the house and then sit inside a public place for long."

"Come on, Christine. We all want to see you. It's just for breakfast. If you can't sit inside, we'll sit outside. Or you can just go back home if you feel you need to leave."

"OK," I conceded. "I'll be there on Thursday morning at ten."

When I hung up the phone, I thought, *I won't be able to sit and listen to conversations about their normal, uninterrupted lives. I'm no longer part of that. My life has ended! . . . But I should get out of the house. I should,* I told myself unconvincingly.

On Thursday, I looked out our living room window at a sunny summer morning. Pink roses and bluebells brightened my neighbor Betsy's front garden. But even the beauty of nature couldn't stop the contradictory thoughts racing through my mind. *I don't want to leave the house, but I told them that I'd come. And I do want to see them. . . . No, I really don't want to talk to anybody.* Despite my confused feelings, I grabbed my car keys and started down the back steps. *Andreas, when will I hear you coming up these stairs again?*

When I arrived at the hotel, I parked my blue Chevy Nova in the lot and waited for my friends. From my car, I noticed the nearby pine trees swaying in the summer breeze. As I sat there, I watched young women and men in lightweight business suits move briskly through the side door of the hotel. *How strange that life is going on as if Andreas wasn't murdered.*

Mary arrived first. When I recognized her sporty, blue Toyota, I reached for the handle of my car door, but then I thought, *I can't go up to her. What am I going to say? How is she going to react to me?* I watched as Mary stepped out of her car. Then I opened my car door, placed my feet on the ground, and, after a few moments, stood on the soft, pine needle-covered path. Fresh morning air engulfed me as I turned my head in every direction before taking small steps toward Mary. *How am I going to greet her? I know I'll start crying and won't be able to stop.*

"Hi, Christine," Mary said in her lively voice. Her auburn hair touched her shoulders, just as it had the last time I'd seen her at work. We put our arms around each other and stood like that for a little while without words. As a faded image of my life in the school system entered my mind, I wondered, *Are Mary, Ruth, and Ros a bridge to my former life? Is this breakfast my first attempt at a potential return? Are they helping me take my first step toward a new life?*

"It's great to see you," Mary said as we stood on the wooded path waiting for Ros and Ruth to arrive. "I'm so glad you came."

Just then, I heard Ros say, "Hi, Christine." She was walking toward me in a pair of familiar blue pants. A gold necklace sparkled against her white blouse, and her short blonde hair framed her round face. We hugged each other in greeting, then she smiled and repeated a few times, "I'm so glad you were able to come. It's so good to see you."

In unison, the two of them repeated, "It's really good to see you, Christine!"

"I'm glad to see you too," I replied. And I meant it. I *was* glad to see them. But at the same time, I was surprised that they or anything else from my life before Andreas's death still existed.

Tireless Ruth, the youngest of our foursome of special education social workers, was last to arrive. I saw her rushing toward us with her typical wide smile, hollering "Hi!" from a distance. But the brightness left her face when we looked into each other's eyes.

The four of us walked in awkward silence toward the hotel door. As we stepped inside, I looked around to make sure I could see every part of the room. *It's so dark in here. Am I safe?* As we followed the hostess to a table, it felt like I was hovering above the ground, not able to feel the floor. We sat down at a square table with a white tablecloth, shiny silverware, and white linen napkins.

I tried to follow the chattering among Mary, Ruth, and Ros, but their words crisscrossed from one person to the other. I strained my ears but couldn't quite decipher the words. My attention was on Andreas. *Does anybody else see him?* I wondered. He was sitting next to me at the table. He loved going out for breakfast when we visited his Oma, Robert's mother, in New Jersey.

At one point, I heard a jumbled sentence, "Remember . . . evaluated . . . hospital . . . head spinning . . . real crazy . . . kids . . . teachers . . . the principal." The words had a distantly familiar sound, but no matter how hard I tried, I could not string them into a coherent sentence. But eventually, I gathered that my friends were talking about some of the challenges they'd faced during the last days of school before summer break, and a shadowy glimpse began to appear, a faint feeling of having once lived the life they were describing. It was then that I realized my world had shrunk. I was spending all my time with Andreas, just as I did right after he was born. Back then, even when he was in his crib in the next room, I could sense him and knew when he needed me. Now, although I could still feel his presence, he was beyond my help. My waking hours and dream-infused nights were filled only with thoughts of him.

I continued to try to follow the discussion at the table, and occasionally, Mary, Ros, and Ruth tried to bring me into their world.

"Christine, sorry we're bitching about the craziness at school," Ros apologized. "As you can probably tell, nothing has changed. We're so glad you were able to make it today! It's really good to see you again."

They spoke about other things, but little they said registered with me. I sensed my friends could no longer find me—that I had changed in some irreversible way. I now belonged to a different world, one in which I would forever carry the pain from the loss of my son and the terrible knowledge of the violent death he suffered. Eventually, they switched to other topics that I could more easily follow.

"We're spending the rest of the summer up in Maine," Ros said with excitement in her voice. "We're leaving in two weeks."

Ruth brightened up the conversation with tales about the latest man in her life. "I met a guy last week," she giggled. "He's real cute."

With her young face beaming, Mary also offered some details about her latest beau. "We're still together. I'm going to meet his sister this summer. That's going to be quite something," she said with a heartfelt laugh.

Their contagious excitement stirred something buried deep inside me. *Life continues. How strange, how comforting.* Yet even as I sensed a fleeting wisp of possibility, I thought to myself, *I can't imagine ever being able to join in again.*

—◌◌—

Saturday, July 15, 1989

Andreas,

Exactly five weeks ago today, you were murdered. My heart still bleeds as I think about how viciously your life was taken from you. I feel guilty because I couldn't keep you safe. I failed to instill fear in you. It might have saved your life.

Andreas, I think of how handsome you looked in your new striped shirt, the one you'd ironed just before you went out with your friends to the carnival. I always loved watching you get ready, especially when you'd iron your clothes. I felt proud knowing you could take care of yourself.

As I write to you now, images of the night you were attacked stream through my mind: I see Mike, Sam, and Todd rushing up our back stairs, their shirts torn and their eyes wide. Mike was breathing hard and speaking rapidly as he handed me your eagle necklace and your torn, bloody jeans. "Andreas was hurt in a fight!" he cried out. "It could've been me or any of us!"

The front doorbell interrupted what your friends were frantically telling me. When I ran to answer it, I was surprised to see your friend Tim with a police officer standing behind him. Tim looked at me, speechless, turned his head toward the young officer, and then looked at me again and handed me your leather wallet. The officer stepped forward with a grave expression on his face as he slowly said, "Andreas was hurt. He's on his way to the hospital by ambulance."

"Is it serious?" I asked.

"Get to the hospital as quickly as possible," was the officer's reply.

As Tim and the officer disappeared into the darkness, I rushed up the stairs to wake your dad. Tom had just come into the kitchen.

Andreas, I sensed that something very bad had happened to you, but it didn't occur to me that I would never see you again. Even after we attempted to find you in the hospital emergency room and the nurse screamed at us, "You can't go in there! I thought he was going to die when he was wheeled in. His eyes had rolled back in his head. The whole emergency room is closed to take care of your son!" I still refused to believe her. I was sure she was wrong. Instead of leading us to you, the nurse opened the big swinging door and directed us to the waiting area where some of your friends had already gathered. Some stood leaning against a wall; one was lying on the floor holding his head in his hands; the others were sitting on benches. Police officers were all around.

Andreas, did any of your friends go with you in the ambulance?

I can't bear the pain of not seeing you anymore.

Loving you always,

Mom

—⟰—

Thursday, July 20, 1989

Andreas,

It's past midnight and five days since I last wrote to you. I don't have words to express how much I still miss you. I can't comprehend that somebody could hurt you so badly. None of us, not even Tom and his friends—who walked by the commotion on the street that night—could protect you. Tom's friend Steve, you remember him, told me how guilty he and Tom felt for not having stopped at the scene. But they didn't know it was you who needed help. Nobody has been able to make sure that the young man accused of your murder is locked up. Your friends tell me that somebody recently saw him playing basketball at the courts. What if he kills someone else?

Andreas, I miss your presence in the kitchen. You naturally knew how to help. I can see your sweet smile as you stir the potato salad with a large spoon.

Today we went to see a family therapist. It felt very strange because there were only three of us in the room. Nobody spoke about you, even though I'd brought the big picture of you in the motorboat, the one Todd took when you were with him on vacation in Maine. The therapist just pointed out how angry we all were. I wanted the therapist to ask us about you, to look at your picture. I needed to tell him what happened.

Miss you still, with a broken heart,

Mom

—m—

Sunday, July 23, 1989

Andreas, it's been six weeks since you were taken from us. Today your dad, Tom, and I went to the airport with Julia. Since the day she accompanied us home from the hospital, after we had to leave you there, she and I have been seeing each other often during her lunch breaks at work near Central Square in Cambridge. We sit in the park and talk, mostly about you and how much she, Mark, and Peter miss you. You, Tom, and her two sons were like brothers. Today Mark returned from his college semester abroad in Kenya. We all went to the airport to pick him up. While waiting for him, I felt like I was waiting for you.

It was nice to see Mark looking so happy as he came through the gate. Yet the moment I hugged him, I was overwhelmed by the realization that I would never again hold you. I will never see you leave me to return a grown man.

Andreas, earlier today I went to be with you at the cemetery. Two of your friends had left red roses. They had tied notes to the flowers and placed them on the freshly planted grass that covers your grave. As I looked at the notes, I could feel my heart tearing into pieces. They confirmed the reality that I will never see you with a girlfriend, married, or with a child of your own.

These letters to you are my lifeline—a continuous way of staying in touch with you. I need to keep writing so that I can at least pretend to be talking to you.

Andreas, life is no longer the same. Now I can see evil much more clearly.

Loving you and missing you forever,

Mom

—⁓—

Sunday, July 30, 1989

Dear Andreas,

I haven't written to you for a few days because I just couldn't take the pen in my hand. I miss you too much every second of every day. Even at night, I wake up almost hourly, and instantly, my thoughts go to you. I can't bear your absence any longer.

Andreas, do you remember my Chilean friend, Regina? She came to visit me this evening. She's going to divinity school to become a pastor. As we talked, she said, "How can God let our children be murdered? I no longer understand anything."

We discussed death. Regina is sure your soul is now free of pain, and she's sure you're still with us. Your death has brought such heartache into our lives yet also an outpouring of love and caring from longtime friends and even strangers. But, of course, I would rather do without that and have you here with me.

Andreas, I want to join you, but what about Tom? He needs to see that I can survive. I can't let the murderer kill yet another member of our family. He's done enough damage already. But I don't know how much longer I can live with this pain. Life is no longer the same here on Earth.

Forever,

Mom

—⁓⁓—

Monday, July 31, 1989

Dear Andreas,

It's midnight, and the house is unbearably quiet. Not a sound comes from your room. I would give anything in the world to see you sitting in front of your stereo, being blasted into another dimension by the sound coming from the speakers. I never understood why the music had to be so loud. Now I don't need to understand. I only wish I could hear your voice once again.

Always thinking of you, still in pain,

Mom

CHAPTER 4

August

In early August, the sound of the ringing phone cut through the heaviness in our house. I didn't want to talk to anybody, but reluctantly, I stepped toward the phone and slowly reached for the receiver. It was Mike's mother.

"Hi. It's Maureen," came the familiar voice tinged with an Irish brogue. "I'd like to take you out to eat. I'll pick you up tomorrow at noon. Is that OK?"

She wants to get me out of the house. What if I can't turn off the tears that long? I thought just before I heard myself respond in a quivering voice, "Yes."

"I was thinking we could go to a seafood restaurant in Arlington. Would you like that?" Before I could answer, she continued, "They have the most delicious lobster pie. It's my favorite. I bet you'll like it too."

At noon the next day, I got into Maureen's Mercury sedan. "It's really nice to see you again," she said as I fastened my seat belt. I had no words, only my tears spoke. "It's hard. It doesn't get any easier with time, does it." It was more a statement of fact than a question.

At the crowded restaurant, I followed Maureen to the hostess stand, which was next to the lounge. "We'd like a booth for two," Maureen requested.

"It'll be about a fifteen-minute wait," the hostess replied, handing Maureen a card with a number on it. As I stood facing Maureen, whose back was to the noisy lounge, I noticed an animated crowd of men and women chatting as they sat in velvety, upholstered chairs around low round tables. Next to them, a smaller group laughed loudly as they sipped their drinks.

"Wait until you taste . . . and the dessert. . . ." Maureen's mouth was moving, but I could only make out part of what she was saying over the din of the crowd. As I turned my head a bit to try to hear her better, I saw a TV in the corner of the lounge set to a station playing a crime show. Images flickering on the screen showed a young man wielding a large knife. It caught me off guard and I quickly turned away, but it was too late to avoid seeing the actor take aim at a screaming young woman. All the while, the men and women in the lounge continued nibbling on appetizers and sipping their cocktails. Some of them chuckled boisterously, while others kept talking.

Doesn't anybody notice the woman screaming? How can people watch this and keep laughing? How can they show something like this in public at a place where people come to relax and eat? I kept trying to concentrate on what Maureen was saying, but I could barely hear her.

"Christine, they just called our number," Maureen said with a smile, pulling me back to the present.

Sitting across from one another on the turquoise benches of the booth, we studied the large menu. I fixed my gaze on the words but couldn't make sense of what I was reading. When the waitress returned a few minutes later and asked if we were ready to order, I just stared at her.

"Would you like me to help you choose something?" Maureen offered.

"You go first," I said, still trying to wipe the images I'd seen on the TV screen from my mind so I could focus on the menu.

Maureen sat upright in anticipation of the waitress taking her order. "I'd like the lobster pie with a baked potato and a salad with blue cheese dressing," she said, her eyes shining brightly.

My mind went blank when the waitress looked my way. "I'll have the same," was all I could say.

When our food first arrived, I only poked at it with my fork, pushing it around the plate. But I had known Maureen for as long as Mike and Andreas had been friends, so after a while, with a feeling of gladness to be in her company, I began to enjoy my meal.

"You know, Andreas loved this dish," Maureen said. "It's so strange not to have him around anymore. It's so hard to comprehend. I still can't believe he's not coming back. He spent a lot of time at our house with Mike. He was always such a sweetheart. I know he's with us right now, but he's in a better place."

Holding back tears, I listened in silence.

Friday, August 4, 1989
Dear Andreas,
On Wednesday I had lunch with Maureen, Mike's mother. She still can't believe you're not coming back.

Yesterday, a woman who I know through work took me to a Buddhist service. The entire time I was with her, she kept telling me that your soul lives on and that, eventually, it will come back to this life in another body. But I don't want you in another body! I want you in *your* body, here at home. I sense that your soul is all around me, and I carry you inside me everywhere I go.

Andreas, death is mysterious. I don't know what to believe, but I do know that as long as I live, you will always be with me. I'll love you forever,
Mom

Sunday, August 6, 1989

Dear Andreas,

It's noon and I'm sitting on a bench in the Boston Common. The familiar and soothing Sunday sounds of church bells ringing echo through the park. A group of young tourists is walking by, stopping to look at the statehouse with its golden dome. I just came from King's Chapel where Reverend Foreman works. He's the minister who officiated at your funeral.

I've been thinking about you all day. You died eight weeks ago. I hear you screaming and see you kneeling, covered with blood and trying to get up from the street to get help. The only consolation I have is that you were with your friends. I hope that, in time, I can feel more of your presence and be able to remember you without so much pain.

Andreas, my therapist will call me tomorrow morning to check in with me. He has been my lifeline, sustaining me from falling into the abyss, even though I sometimes want to let go so I can join you. But first I will find some way to give meaning to your suffering, to bear witness so others may learn from it. Andreas, can you give me strength from wherever you are?

I just thought of another thing I want to tell you. Yesterday your dad, Tom, and I went to a cookout at Julia's house for the first time without you. My heart tore apart when I saw Peter and Tom playing Frisbee against Mark and his friend Sean. If you were still alive, you would've been Mark's partner instead of Sean. It was always you, Tom, Peter, and Mark. You would've been the one to light the grill. This time your brother did it.

Julia was also sad. The night before, she'd seen a tiny kitten on the side of the street on her way home from work. She said the kitten reminded her of how gentle you were. She remembered you and the fun you had playing with your little black cat.

Andreas, I still miss you terribly and hope and pray that you are still with me. I need to believe that you're not gone forever. The pain of your absence is unbearable.

Love you forever,

Mom

—⟐—

Wednesday, August 9, 1989

Dear Andreas,

It's two o'clock in the morning, and I can't sleep. I just want to tell you that Regina came again today. She asked me to type a paper for her on my computer. But once I was finished, the printer refused to cooperate. You can imagine how furious we were. Her paper is due this morning at nine, so I had to retype everything on your typewriter. I didn't want to use it, but it was the only option. As I worked, I thought of how, just a few months ago, I watched as you did your homework, your nimble fingers moving across the same keys.

Andreas, something feels strange. You left your things behind. Did you forget to take them?

I still love and miss you every minute of every day,

Mom

—⟐—

Friday, August 11, 1989

Andreas,

It's two thirty in the afternoon. Earlier today, I placed some scarlet-red gladiolus on your grave. You would love them and the salmon-colored lilies Tom put there a few days ago. I remember how much you liked fresh flowers on our dining room table.

Andreas, I've been reading books about life after death. I want to believe that life after death exists because it would mean that you're with me still. But I miss you. Outside my window, it's a dark and rainy day. Even the sky cries for you.
Thinking of you with all my love,
Mom

—⁊⁊—

Saturday, August 19, 1989
Andreas,
It's two o'clock on Saturday morning, and I'm wide awake. I've been feeling enraged about what happened to you. How could anybody take a huge kitchen knife, stab you, punch you, and then, as if that weren't enough, beat your head with a heavy stick? And now, the person accused of doing this to you is out on bail, moving freely among us.

Andreas, earlier today I talked to my Aunt Martha and her son, Manfred, in West Germany and to my cousin Angelika in East Germany. They told me that they're all still in shock over your death. They can't believe that something like this could happen in America. Tante Martha kept repeating, "Das gibt's doch nicht bei Euch in Amerika. Das gibt's doch nicht!" ("This can't be in America. It can't be!")

Manfred, who is a police officer, told me that their whole village is outraged. They are all trying to make sense of it. He angrily asked, "Wie kann so etwas passieren?" ("How can something like that happen?")

My cousin Angelika was sick for three weeks after hearing the news. She almost had a nervous breakdown! So many people are in shock and unable to absorb what happened to you.

Andreas, I'm going to try to sleep now. But I keep thinking of you.

Loving you always, my dear son,
Mom
P.S. Your dad and I are thinking of getting a headstone for your burial place with an engraving of the sun—to represent the warmth, love, light, and beauty you gave us—and a cross for the torturous way in which you were killed.

—ɷ—

Sunday, August 20, 1989
My dear Andreas,
In my search to find answers for your violent death, I went to a Quaker Friends meeting. I didn't know anyone there. I felt a little nervous but just followed the lead of the others and took a seat around the circle. Not wanting to invite conversation, I kept a neutral expression on my face and cast my eyes downward. In this way, I felt I would be an invisible presence. Since your death, I've come to this lonely way of being. It feels safer and prevents me from having to muster energy I really don't have to engage in conversation that has no meaning to me.

While sitting in the circle in silence, I thought only of you. A young woman and an older man in the circle sang spontaneously. The depth of their feelings gave me goose bumps. I wished for a voice to come through me, but all I felt was the pain of your never-ending absence.
Love you always,
Mom

—ɷ—

Monday, August 21, 1989
My dear Andreas,
Right now, I'm sitting at your grave in awe of death. How powerful! Having your life drawn out of you in one brief moment is

inexplicable to me. I cannot let myself comprehend the enormity of this tragedy without falling into a bottomless black hole with nothing there to catch me.

But I also want to tell you something your dad, Tom, and I did yesterday. It was the first time we went out to dinner without you. We went to Demos, remember the Greek restaurant in Watertown? It felt very awkward when the waiter led us to a table set for four. Right after he signaled for us to take our seats, he removed what should've been your place setting, swiftly gathering up the napkin, plate, silverware, and water glass and leaving the tabletop in front of the fourth chair empty. When the food came, none of us felt like eating.

After we finished our meal, the silent pain we all felt but were unable to express was palpable. Tom has decided to attend UMass Amherst, so we chatted about what he still needs to get done before leaving. As we were talking, I thought of how you preferred not to dawdle much in a restaurant once the meal was done. Now I would give anything in the world to hear your steady voice trying once again to gently nudge us out the door after we'd lingered too long. "Come on, Mom and Dad! Let's go. We've been here long enough." I can still fill oceans with my tears.

I love you always,
Mom

—⁊⁊—

Thursday, August 24, 1989
Andreas, Julia's boys, Mark and Peter, stopped by the house yesterday. Mark told us about his time in Kenya and how daily life there is so very different from life in America. You would've loved listening to his stories. This was the first time Mark and I had an opportunity to speak privately since your death, so we stood apart from the others for a bit. Something he said has left

me thinking about life, death, and invisible communication. Mark told me that he'd had a dream on the night you were killed, and in the dream, he saw doctors in an operating room. They were using an instrument to suction blood out of a person's chest. Many people came and went from the room. Then, still in the dream, he heard Peter whisper, "He's dead." Mark said he'd never had a dream like that before, and it frightened him. It wasn't until a few days later that Peter called Mark to let him know what had happened to you.

Mark's dream gave me a little consolation. It made me wonder if your soul was communicating with him, and it reassured me that you did not leave this world alone. You and Mark were like brothers to each other.

Mark told me something else. Shortly after he returned to Boston, he'd gone to a bar one Saturday night with Peter and some friends. At one point while they were talking, another patron became inexplicably angry and smashed a bottle over Mark's head. His friends rushed him to the hospital—the same hospital where, two months earlier at exactly the same hour, medics wheeled you into the emergency room. Luckily, Mark only needed stitches and was able to walk out of the hospital and go home.

Andreas, I still miss you every second of the day.
Loving you always,
Mom

—⁓—

Friday, August 25, 1989
Andreas,
We've been having some gorgeous weather with brilliant blue skies and perfect temperatures. These late summer days remind me of when you, Tom, and I used to go apple picking in early autumn with Julia, Peter, and Mark. We'd stop at their apart-

ment in West Acton for lunch before heading over to nearby Stow. As soon as we arrived at the apple orchard, you and your brother would hop out of the car and race toward the trees with Mark and Peter in tow. I loved seeing the four of you joyfully darting in and out of the long orchard rows and under tree branches that were hanging low and laden with fruit. You and Tom would clamber up the strategically placed ladders and pluck the prettiest pieces of fruit. Then, as if holding a delicate glass snow globe, together you would pass the red apples down to me, one after the other, to keep them from falling to the ground and bruising.

Later, at home, I would bake an apple cake from a recipe in my old German cookbook. The smells from the kitchen would mingle with the sounds of laughter as you played with your brother, contented, warm, and cozy.

Thinking of you always and with love,

Mom

Saturday, August 26, 1989

Andreas,

On this late summer evening, I sat on our porch, feeling the cool breeze brush against my cheeks. The change of temperature made it clear that the summer stole you away from me. Moving on to the next season will be like extricating myself from a mangled car and leaving you behind.

Today while your dad was at home working, I went to the cemetery to visit you. Mesmerized by the beauty of the leaves of the katsura trees as they fluttered in the wind near your grave, I suddenly felt totally alive and at one with nature—the trees, the birds, the sky—despite the harsh reality that your young body lay buried beneath this heavenly landscape. You're no longer able to perceive such beauty. Or can you? Andreas, I want to go back to that summer night and stop time. You'll still be out with your friends having fun at the fair, and I'll be at home waiting with the certainty that you'll walk through the door.

I miss you and will always love you.

Mom

—⁓—

Tuesday, August 29, 1989

My dear Andreas,

It's a little after three o'clock in the afternoon, and I just got home after spending a night with my friend Kathy and her girls at a seaside hotel in Maine. Remember Kathy? She was my roommate when I first came to Boston in 1966, long before you were born. But later, she got married and moved to Manchester, New Hampshire. We used to go there to visit her when you and Tom were young, and Kathy would always have some freshly baked brownies for us. For yesterday's visit in Maine, I went alone. If you were still here, I'm sure you and Tom would've come along, and the mood would've been lively and fun. But this time, my visit with them felt vastly different. In the morning, I felt hollow inside as I sat alone, listening to the sound of the rippling waves and watching the sun rise above the water. I thought of how much you loved the ocean and going for rides in Todd's motorboat not far from here.

On the way home, I drove to Nashua, New Hampshire. Todd had organized a cookout there in your memory, and he asked me to stop by. He told me that he'd invited some of your college friends and that Tom and Peter also planned to be there. But after I found the house tucked away in the woods at the end of a long dirt road, I stayed hidden in my car behind a row of bushes. When I saw Todd and the others standing around a grill and talking, I became too nervous to get out of my car. I didn't hear any music, but seeing the group of young men made me think of how much fun you'd once had with these friends and your brother. Watching them, I could only feel your absence. Not wanting to make them uncomfortable, I sat there for a while then turned my car around and headed back down the dirt road.

Although I was headed for home, I decided to first stop by the cemetery. As I stood by your grave, I wanted to scream and never stop. I wanted to stomp on the ground and kick everything in sight. But I had to remain calm because there were other visitors nearby, and I feared they'd suspect I'd lost my mind. Sometimes, it feels as if I have.

Love you always,

Mom

—ɷ—

Wednesday, August 30, 1989

My dear Andreas,

I just want to share with you what I'm seeing. It's late afternoon as I sit on the soft grass next to your grave. The leaves on the trees around you are dancing to the rhythm of the warm, gentle breeze. The late summer sun's golden orb softly illuminates a cornflower-blue sky; its slanted rays shine through the pine trees, creating reflections of light and shade all around your grave. I want you to see this earthly beauty. Please, Andreas, can you be with me to see it?

Andreas, it's time for me to go home now. It's getting late and Julia is coming over for dinner.

I think of you always and love you forever,

Mom

CHAPTER 5

Back to Work

Yesterday at the cemetery, I watched a yellow leaf fall onto Andreas's grave. It reminded me that school would soon resume, and I would return to work. *Please time, can you rewind or at least keep Andreas's scent, his voice, his smile fresh in my memory? I need to return to work. But is there any going back? Wasn't the return bridge blown up? How can I reconnect with where I left off in my life as if nothing has happened? Andreas is gone. He'll never return. But I know I must find a way to piece things together and connect my past with my new beginning.*

While imagining going back to schools where teachers, principals, and students still exist, I was surprised to discover a bright thread, like the wick of a flickering candle, that was still alive in the rubble of my heart. Yet I could not imagine returning to work at a busy school as if nothing had changed. Many questions ran through my head: *How can I bridge the abyss that now separates me from the teachers, principals, counselors, and the once familiar buildings? How can I start school and pick up where I left off, knowing there's an infinite gulf between my last day at work and now? Will I be able to keep my tears at bay when I see colleagues who knew me before the night of June 10, when Andreas's friends ran up our back stairs to tell me that he was hurt? Will I be able to handle the frequent images my mind has conjured of the murder, which seem to have a schedule of their own? Can I still do my job working with children in the schools? And if there's a trial, will I be able to attend?*

The prosecutor, Mr. Rapacki, had made it clear to Robert and me that our presence in the courtroom was crucial if there was a trial. "It's important for the judge and jury to see the parents and as many family members as can attend the trial. It shows that Andreas was part of a family who cared about him."

On the last day of August, I climbed behind the wheel of my car and headed to one of the middle schools I worked at to meet with the principal to discuss my worries about returning to work. *I need to do this,* I thought. *I can't just appear on the first day of school when everybody will be there.* It was an easy commute, and when I arrived, the parking lot in front of the middle school was practically empty. I sat in my car for a bit, staring at the bright yellow entrance. Eventually, I pushed open the door because I knew Nestor and Max, the principal and vice principal, were waiting for me. But before locking the car door, I looked all around, checking to make sure I was safe.

Once inside the high-ceilinged front hall, I took a quick right turn, passed by the receptionist's desk, and knocked softly on the windowpane of the principal's office door. Nestor, a slender man about my height, immediately stood up from behind his desk and waved me in.

As we looked at each other for a moment, I could see tears teetering on the base of his eyelids. "I'm deeply sorry about your son, Christine. May God's love help you bear the pain," he said as he put his arms around me. Instantly, the chasm that I felt before entering his office shrank.

Soon, Max, the vice principal, joined us. He, too, embraced me and said, "May God's love comfort you." His words turned on a light in my heart. *Andreas, are you the light? Are you with God?*

The three of us took seats around Nestor's desk, a place where we'd sat many times before as we'd watched parents shed tears while lamenting, "I don't know what to do with my son anymore."

After our meeting ended, I stopped at the receptionist's desk. Bonnie also gave me a hug and added, "It's wonderful to see you. And I'm glad you're coming back. Go walk around the school a little."

A large empty hallway with a polished concrete floor led me toward the classrooms. I took my time, walking slowly as my hands brushed against the rough brick walls.

I made my way inside a classroom and ran my hand over the familiar smooth tops of the students' desks and listened to the silence that, in just a few days, would be replaced with lively chatter. At that moment, I knew in my heart that I could face the upcoming school year and return to the work I loved.

Thursday, August 31, 1989
Andreas,
I just visited the principals at the middle school where I will start working again next week. It's four thirty in the afternoon, and I'm at the park in Lincoln, sitting on a patch of grass beside the small pond. You know the place. It's another bright, sunny day, yet the late summer breeze hints of autumn. The leaves are turning, and some have a yellow shimmer. Time is visibly passing, pulling you further away from me.

Like an old home-movie reel, I see flashing images of everything you used to do at this time of year: the back-to-school rituals of stocking up on school supplies and shopping at the mall with your friends for new sneakers or jeans or maybe a backpack. You won't do any of those things this year. Where are you? Where have you gone?

Andreas, remember how you and Tom used to play Frisbee on this field when we'd visit the park? Now I watch as a family of five ducks waddle along not far from where I sit. The parents and their little ones repeatedly poke their bills into the soft earth looking for food. Whenever a duck from another family tries to move into their territory, they attack and chase it away. But no one is stabbed; no one is killed for intruding into their space.

Andreas, I will stop at the jewelry repair shop to pick up my watch—a gift to me from your Opa many years ago. Inexplicably, the watch stopped running the night you died. I want the comforting feel of it back on my wrist, its thin silver hands ticking like a beating heart.

Andreas, I miss you and love you always,

Mom

—⚶—

Saturday, September 2, 1989

Andreas,

Yesterday your dad and I went to see Mr. Rapacki. Every time we meet with him, I feel confused. I still don't understand the legal maneuvering he talks about. He said the trial will start on September 11, but there might not be a trial. If there is a trial, he said it's important for us to be there. He also said the accused might still accept a plea bargain. As I understand it, that means he'll admit to committing the crime. Then the judge will decide how long he needs to spend in jail. It's so confusing, Andreas. I don't know what I want other than for all of this to end and for you to come home. That's all.

Andreas, our victim advocate, Lucy, showed us the courtrooms. I can't imagine sitting in one of those rooms and seeing the one who is accused of causing you such unimaginable pain. It's beyond what my heart can take. Doing so would mean you're really gone and that what we've been told happened to you is true. The doctor who tried to save your life will testify. It's going to be strange to see him. Will it take me back to that Saturday night? Can he change the outcome of your surgery?

Andreas, I feel that I failed you terribly as a mother. I brought you into this world but did not give you the necessary tools to survive in it.

I miss you and constantly think of you, Andreas.

I love you forever.

Mom

—⁓—

On Tuesday, September 5, just a few days after my meeting with Nestor and Max, I left home and drove along the tree-lined turnpike, which was enveloped in the glorious colors of autumn. It was the first official day of the school year for staff members. I headed away from my usual assigned schools toward an elementary school in a different district. It was at this school, with its auditorium large enough to hold teachers and staff, that I would attend the superintendent's traditional welcome back ceremony. *I'm going back to my normal life. Why, then, do I feel this trembling in my body? Am I not just going back to work as I usually do in the fall?*

How will my coworkers and the students react to me? Will they feel awkward in my presence? Will they avoid me? Will I avoid them? Will what they say hurt me? Will I be able to withstand the many greetings and questions about how I'm doing? Will I be able to get through the day without crying, without thinking of Andreas?

I soon arrived at the crowded parking lot of Brown Elementary School, where only staff members were present that day. After shutting off the engine, I remained hidden among the sea of cars and stared out the window. My body felt heavy. *I wish I had stayed home. I don't want to go in there. Andreas, are you with me? Should I go in and listen to the superintendent's welcome back speech? No, I think I'll stay outside and wait for the ceremony to end.*

But after a few minutes, I decided that I needed to go in. *Maybe Ros, Ruth, and Mary are there, and I can sit with them.* With a new sense of determination, I approached the side entrance of the large auditorium, pulled the handle of the heavy door, and opened it a crack, just enough to take a quick peek inside. Like carelessly flung rocks, out came the voices of reunited colleagues: "You look fabulous!" "I had a great summer!"

Gasping for air, I quickly pushed the door shut. Taking a few steps away from the building, I stopped and gazed up at the pale blue sky, then silently pleaded, *Andreas, please be with me.* In response, a trio of puffy white clouds passed overhead. Deliberately slowing my breath in hopes of calming myself, I tried again to join the crowd. This time when I opened the door, I saw that everybody had taken a seat. I made a beeline for the closest empty chair and sat down. Soon, the superintendent stepped onto the stage. Bending his neck down toward the microphone, he began, "Welcome back! I hope you all had a great summer!"

As the crowd cheered exuberantly, I tried hard not to allow his words to reach my heart. I didn't want the images of my summer becoming too vivid in my mind.

While I held on tightly to the armrest of my chair, he continued. "I hope you all had the opportunity to replenish your energy and have come back recharged and ready to face another challenging school year. With your strength and courage, we'll make this year another great learning experience for our children."

Please let my life go back to normal. Please, . . . please! I want to be one of the crowd again. Andreas, please, you must come home!

The rest of the day was a blur, but I do have a distinct memory of standing next to Andreas's grave later in the day and silently asking him, *Can you please give me strength for tomorrow when the children return to school?*

The next day, I again sped down the highway. *Do the students know why I left so abruptly before the end of the last school year? How will they react when they see me? How will I react to them?* I arrived at the elementary school on that foggy September morning as rows of second grade boys and girls with bright new book bags were meandering down the corridor. Some of the young students' faces sparkled with a special back-to-school smile, glad to be reunited with their friends.

I remember when Andreas . . . , I started to think but then quickly halted such thoughts. *Stop! Don't think about Andreas now. Concentrate on just being here.*

When I got to my office, my heart was pounding so rapidly that it felt like it was vibrating off the freshly painted cabbage-white walls. I calmed myself by grabbing a paper towel and wiping a summer's worth of dust off my desk and the children's table and chairs. After placing newly sharpened colored pencils, small stacks of paper, and UNO game cards on the table, I felt a strange sense of déjà vu. Next, I hung a picture of a blooming yellow araguanay tree that reminded me of Venezuela. Just as I was trying to figure out where to hang my world map, I heard a familiar voice call out, "Hola, Christina!" I turned around and saw my office neighbor, Maria, the friendly guidance counselor. Her hair was secured with a red clip, her long, black locks flowing down her back. As we briefly gazed into each other's eyes, I sensed something between us that had never been there before. When we hugged, I squeezed my eyes tight to keep the tears from trickling down my face. *I'm at work now. I mustn't cry.*

Later that morning, I went to meet with Ms. Jane, the head of my department, regarding the need for time off should there be a trial. The usually vibrant woman greeted me in a subdued manner. "I am so sorry about what happened to your son," she said with compassion in her eyes.

I tried very hard not to cry. I feared that if I started sobbing at work, my boss would think I could no longer do my job. Eventually, after some small talk, I broached the subject that had brought me to her office. "There's most likely going to be a trial, and the prosecuting attorney has stressed how important it is for my husband and me to be there. The trial is scheduled to start on Monday, but it might start later. I don't know how long it will last. It could be anywhere from one to three weeks. What do I need to do to take time off to attend the trial?"

I hoped to hear Ms. Jane say, "Of course, Christine, you can take as long as you need to attend the trial of your son's murderer. I know how important that is to you. This is the chance to witness the last moments of your son's life. I know you couldn't say goodbye."

But instead, Ms. Jane's tight-lipped reply was hesitant. "I can't tell you right away. I'll have to discuss it with the superintendent. I'll let you know in a few days. In the meantime, fill out the personal leave form and send it to me."

I felt short of breath but managed to choke out a polite reply, "Thank you for your time." I left her office in a daze but made my way to the parking lot. *Why must I beg for time off to seek justice for my son? Time off to attend legal proceedings—proceedings that could hold Andreas's killer accountable? Proceedings that might prevent the murderer from taking another life?* I wanted to kick everything around me, lash out and never stop. Confused, hurt, disappointed, and angry, I exited the building and headed to the middle school where I was working that afternoon. The drive gave me time to think. *Calm down, Christine,* I reasoned with myself. *You have to go back to work.*

At the middle school, I heard children's lively voices coming from the classrooms as I moved swiftly down the long corridor toward my office. Before I reached my desk, I ran into Marilyn, a fellow social worker. She gave me a warm hug and ushered me into her office where she asked, "How are you doing, Chris?"

"I'm doing alright . . . just trying to get used to being back. Do you know what the students in Ms. Bui's class were told about why I left so abruptly toward the end of the school year?"

"I'm not sure. I guess they were told you had a family crisis."

"What do you think I should tell them when they ask me, especially the boys I was seeing regularly?"

"Just tell them you had a death in the family. They might not even ask. You know these kids have so many problems of their own."

"I guess you're right. I'll see how it goes."

"Chris, what's up with the case? Did they catch him yet?"

"Yes, they caught him. But he's out on bail. The trial is going to start next Monday, but if he accepts a plea bargain, it won't even go to trial. It's so confusing. I hope I can get time off from work so I can attend the court proceedings."

As I left Marilyn's office, she offered, "If you ever need to talk or cry, just come see me."

A few minutes later, I looked in on Ms. Bui's classroom. "Chris, when are you going to start seeing Dan again?" Ms. Bui asked. "School has just started, and he's already causing trouble in the classroom."

"I could see him tomorrow if you'd like. Do you have his parents' approval?"

"Oh, yes. They want help for their son."

"OK," I said. "I'll go visit his parents in the morning to see what they can tell me about how Dan's summer went and what their concerns are."

On my way home after the first day of school, I stopped at the cemetery, pulling my car close to the spot that gave me the best view of Andreas's grave. With various colorful autumn flowers in full bloom and fragrant tall pines standing by, I picked up the lined notebook that rested next to me on the passenger seat and began to write.

Wednesday, September 6, 1989
Dear Andreas,
It's likely that the trial will start on Monday. I'm so afraid to hear all the details of what happened to you on that night. I

can't imagine strangers talking about you in legal, objective language. Will they also bring alive your gentle personality? I hope I can hold up.

Andreas, I don't have a lot of words right now. Fear is strangling my feelings and thoughts.
Still loving you forever,
Mom

—ᴍ—

Andreas,
It's evening now, and I'm writing you another letter—two in one day. Lucy, the victim advocate, called us a little while ago. She told us that the trial has been postponed. There's still a possibility that there won't even be a trial. The one I can't even think of as being human, your accused murderer, might still accept a plea bargain. When I heard that, my heart sank. I pictured him going to jail for a few years, and then, as if nothing had happened, walking the streets again, ready to kill someone else, possibly even one of us. Then Lucy said that if there is a trial and he's found not guilty, he would walk free right away. There's always a chance that the prosecuting attorney might not be able to convince the jurors that he committed the crime.

I'm very confused, Andreas. Part of me wants a trial, and part of me doesn't. What I want most of all is for this nightmare to end and for you to come home. I want to see you curled up on our living room sofa, listening to your favorite music on your headphones. Andreas, I want to know why someone would kill and for what reason you had to sacrifice your young life. And for that, there must be a trial.
Love you forever, Andreas,
Your despairing mom

As a liaison social worker between home and school, I was eager to return to my work in the community where many of the students I served lived. It was a low-income area of hardworking parents who were eager for their children to do well; sadly, many of these students had difficulties concentrating in school. Most families faced tremendous stress related to financial insecurity, health factors, violence in the community, or a history of violence in their communities of origin. Having experienced similar conditions as a German national and refugee growing up in Venezuela, I recognized some of the hurdles they faced daily.

My world had again become a dangerous place. The actions of a young man with a large kitchen knife and a heavy wooden stick had destroyed my illusion of safety—a fantasy that I'd built up in my mind after Tom and Andreas were born. On one home visit before Andreas was killed, I'd seen a large American flag hanging on the living room wall with a photo of a young soldier next to it. In another home, a candle burned steadily beside a statue of the Virgin Mary and photos of their young son. I had seen these things and met these families, but had their losses penetrated any deeper than the outer layer of my heart?

After my own son's violent death, I joined these families in creating shrines to my beloved. I, too, lit candles and placed bouquets of miniature pink roses alongside a large photo of Andreas in our dining room. Since his death, I was no longer a sympathetic observer of the pain and sorrow violence causes. I could suddenly feel that soul-crushing sorrow deep in my own bones.

On my first home visit of the new school year, I stopped at the Vega residence. Dan, his parents, and his two older brothers lived in the low-income area not far from the school Dan attended. Because I'd spoken with his mother on the phone the day before, I knew she didn't have the means to come to the school for a meeting, so I stopped in at their home on the way to my office. I also knew that Dan's mother was eager to speak with me since we'd worked together during the previous school year to help her son.

Upon my arrival, I was greeted by Mrs. Vega, a diminutive woman with short salt-and-pepper hair and curls that loosely hugged her sad, somber face. Gesturing for me to enter the modest apartment, we exchanged a quick hug before taking our seats. I settled into the worn but comfortable living room sofa as she took a chair across from me. A black leather Bible sat on the small coffee table next to her. Kindly, I asked, "How are you? How was your summer?"

Her eyes filled with tears as she met my gaze. Momentarily speechless, she began to cry as she lamented, "I don't know what to do anymore. I've been sick since the beginning of the summer. The doctor told me I have cancer. Dan used to help me around the house. Now he's out all day and night. I don't know what he does or where he goes. We try to get him to stay home, but he doesn't listen to us. My husband is no help. He's drinking again, which is no good for our sons. I hope Dan isn't giving you trouble in school already. I don't know what to do with him anymore," she repeated as her tears continued to fall. "Can you do something with him in school?"

Dan was a tall and handsome seventh grader with hazelnut-colored hair and blue eyes. Because he'd struggled with learning difficulties all his life, he'd been placed in special education classes. His contagious smile and outgoing personality made him very popular among his friends. But in class, he found it difficult to focus, even though he wanted to learn. Anxiety and shame overcame him whenever the teacher asked him to read because he was unable to do so. He yearned to become a professional athlete so he could give his mother a better life.

The next day, I met with Dan at school. He appeared to be glad to see me; I could tell by his smile and his easy willingness to leave the classroom to come to my office. After settling into a chair across from me at the blue children's table, he ignored the UNO cards and colored pencils that before summer vacation had captured his attention. Then he began to tell me, in a voice that was barely audible, of experiences he'd had over the summer months. "We hung out at the tracks in the evenings and waited for trains. One time, this other kid tied a little kitten to the track. It screeched and wiggled a lot. We wanted to see what would happen when the wheels ran it over. It went *whoomp!* The train left it flat." Dan laughed sheepishly, knowing that the story was affecting me. Perhaps my face revealed the horror I felt because he added, almost as an afterthought, "No, we didn't really do that."

I began to feel dizzy as I wondered about Andreas's murderer. *Was this what his life had been like? Did he, too, have nothing better to do over summer vacation than hang out with other bored kids and cause trouble?*

After a short, awkward silence, Dan's face became profoundly serious, almost menacing. "I know you think I killed your son," he blurted out, catching me off guard.

"What makes you think that?" I asked, trying not to show my nervousness.

"I saw it on TV. Somebody killed him, and you think I did it."

I remained speechless for a moment, not knowing how to respond. After a while I asked, "*You?* Why would I think *you* did it?"

"Because you think I'm bad," he said with conviction.

"Why would I think that about you?" When he didn't respond, I continued, "Dan, I know painful things have happened to you, but that doesn't make you bad."

Dan rested his head on his arms, which were folded on the tabletop. From that position, he looked at me out of the corner of his eye.

"You didn't kill my son, Dan. The boy who did is much older than you, and he lives in a different city," I replied, trying hard not to let my voice quiver.

Dan sat up again and looked at me in silence as if surprised that I was still sitting with him at the table. Then, leaning back in his chair, he asked, "Why did they kill him? Was he in a gang? Did he sell drugs?"

"No, he wasn't in a gang, and he didn't sell drugs. Horrible things can happen to any of us. I know you've had many bad experiences that weren't your fault."

Dan's brow furrowed as he lowered his eyes and fixed his gaze toward the floor. "I'm sorry," he said, twisting his fingers. His voice full of emotion, he looked up at me. As our eyes met, he asked, "Do you cry like my mother? She cries about my cousin who was killed."

Friday, September 8, 1989
Andreas,
I'm back at the duck pond in Lincoln. The late summer sun is warming my face. The leaves on the oak trees are beginning to turn a tawny brown. Fall is clearly on its way, although the sun still radiates the warmth of summer. It's Friday, and I made it through my first week back at work. But yesterday, I truly wondered if I could go on anymore. I felt like a heavy hammer was hitting my heart. Then last night, I had a dream about you, my first one since you left us.

In the dream, you were speaking from behind a closed emergency room door. A young doctor in a white coat stood outside and very matter-of-factly said, "He's dead." But then the door opened, and I saw you, smiling and sitting up on a cot, dressed in your familiar gray jeans and a T-shirt. My heart instantly felt warmed seeing you alive; I was happy that the doctor was wrong. You had small puncture holes in your arms from all the needles they used during your surgery, but you spoke softly and seemed at ease. I don't remember what you said, but at that moment, as I looked upon your tender smile,

my heart felt unburdened, and a tremendous wave of relief
came over me.
Loving you always, my dear son,
Mom

—m—

Monday, September 11, 1989
My dear Andreas,
The trial, which has been postponed, should have begun today.
Instead, we anxiously await news from the court. It's hard not
knowing what will come next or when.

Tom went to UMass Amherst this past weekend to start
school. He decided to transfer there to be closer to home. As I
sit next to your grave site, rays of sunlight break through hazy
clouds overhead. Judging by the melodious chirps and trills I
hear all around me, the birds seem to be having a special celebration. Is it for you? I've never heard them chatter so much,
back and forth from tree to tree. Do they know something I
don't? Are they telling me that you're here with me?

Andreas, something strange happened last week after we
helped Tom move into his dorm. Your dad and I took Tom out
to eat at a restaurant on campus. After the three of us sat down,
a tall waiter with dark brown hair like yours brought us menus.
He handed one to your dad, one to Tom, and one to me, then he
stood next to us in silence for a moment before he slowly walked
away. I couldn't help but let my gaze follow him across the room.
For a moment, he seemed to become you in the way he moved
and carried himself.

A little later, I watched him pour water into our three
glasses while a fourth glass remained unused atop the table in
front of the empty chair that should've been yours. The waiter
appeared a bit nervous as he wrote down our orders—cheese-

burgers for your dad and brother and a pasta dish for me. After
a while, he brought us some crackers and cheese and tall glasses
of Sprite.

While we waited for our food, your dad and I chatted with
Tom and tried to hide our sadness about dropping him off at
that huge campus. Tom will be alone now. He will never get the
opportunity to invite you to stay in his dorm room for a weekend or introduce you to the new friends he'll make at college. He
will never again spend spring or summer breaks with you or
share holidays together.

I wish I could take away Tom's pain, but I don't know how.
Each one of us is bearing the anguish of forever missing you and
carrying the trauma of your violent death in our own way. Having grown up with the hidden pain of our parents, who suffered
so much during World War II, your father and I have few words
of comfort but rather have learned to show our love by being
there for one another. And so today, we are being there for Tom
and doing our best to help him remain steady as he continues
with his education, despite our collective anguish.

When the waiter brought our food, I watched how he leaned
over and gently put a plate in front of each of us. I kept yearning
for it to be you in your life on campus. I imagined that we hadn't
seen you all summer because you were living at the university,
still trying to decide if you wanted to be a chef like you were
debating before you were forced to leave us.

We ate without much appetite, just out of duty to our hungry bellies. Shortly after we took our last bites, the waiter again
came to our table. "Are you finished? May I take your plates?
Would anyone like dessert?"

"No thanks," the three of us replied in unison.

"Just the check please," your dad added.

When the waiter returned with the check, your dad placed his credit card inside the folder with the bill. A few minutes later, when the young waiter returned with the credit card in his hand, he stood beside our table in silence for a moment, his face pensive. Very slowly, he looked at us and spoke softly. "I'm Theo," he began. "I was on the junior varsity basketball team with Andreas at Belmont High School."

My face lit up and my heart jumped with delight. I wanted this young man to stay with us, sit down at our table, and tell us more, but instead, I asked him what he was doing at the university. He told us he was studying culinary arts, and his job as a waiter was part of his training. Andreas, I wish you were there with Theo telling me about your studies too.

"He was a good kid," Theo said, closing his eyes. A shadow crossed his face and he inhaled deeply. As his eyes fluttered open, I could see that they were moist. He turned his head and looked away.

Andreas, the sun has disappeared behind dark clouds, and now I'm alone in the cemetery. It's very still. Even the birds are silent now.

Always,
Mom

—✗—

September 12, 1989
Andreas,
I'm at your grave again. It's Tuesday.

The moment I left school today, I had a sinking feeling in the pit of my stomach when I realized I wouldn't see you when I got home. There wouldn't even be a phone call from you. I knew I was going home to an empty house; only the cat is there to keep me company now. But since you were taken from us, Fluff looks at me differently. She doesn't greet me at the door when I come home like she used to. Now she just wants to eat constantly, yet she gains no weight.

Andreas, I want to lash out at everything around me. What happened to you makes me want to die, so I can join you. I can't take this life anymore. Andreas, I'm sorry to burden you as if you were an adult, but you probably know that I'm going crazy. I can't go on. I'm close to collapsing. I don't know who to call, who to talk to. I have no more energy to reach out. Where are you, Andreas? Is there really a God who is with you? Can I be sure that your soul is still alive? Why, then, all this pain, Andreas? Are you feeling it as well? Why can't I get a message from you that you're OK and confirmation that I will see you again once I get out of this body?

Andreas, I'm going to water the pot of mums on your grave and check your vase of yellow roses.

Love you forever. See you soon, my dear son.

Mom

P.S. I would feel bad for Tom if I were to leave this life to join you.

On Wednesday, September 13, I was working in one of the elementary schools where I'd already met with a few students. At lunchtime, before going to the teacher's lounge to eat my sandwich, I decided to stop at the front office to check my mailbox. There, I found an official-looking envelope. I carried it back to my office, intuiting that this would be the answer to my request for time off to attend the trial. Sitting down at my desk, I used scissors to cut a thin line along the top of the envelope. My fingers trembled and thoughts raced through my head. *Please let me wake up, please. Please make the threat of a forthcoming*

trial disappear, I begged while carefully pulling out the letter typed on school stationery. "You are approved to take your three personal days consecutively," I read. "You can also take all your sick days. If you need more days off, you need to take them as leave without pay." The letter in my hand became almost too heavy to hold.

I must *be at the trial,* I thought. *I cannot be working while the truth about what happened to Andreas is revealed in court. I want to know why that young man killed him! Mr. Rapacki already said that our presence at the trial will be extremely important. But what if I need a day off during the year? I know I'm going to need a break to help keep up my strength, and what if I get sick?*

After lunch, I walked down the corridor of the middle school where I'd worked that afternoon. I remembered Marilyn's offer, so I knocked on her door. "What's the matter, Chris?" she asked. I showed her the letter and released a torrent of tears. "I can't believe it!" she responded, staring at the letter in her hand.

"Again, it's the victim who must carry the whole burden! I lost my son in a cruel and violent manner, and now I'll lose my income. I don't want to lose my job—I know I can still do my work—but I need those days off to attend the trial! Robert had no problem at his job. Without hesitation, his boss asked him how long he needed to be out. They gave him time off *with pay* and without having to take any personal days—as if he simply has jury duty. Why can't the school do the same for me?"

"Chris, why don't you speak to Ms. Jane again? Maybe she didn't realize how much it means for you to attend the trial. I'm so sorry you have to go through this."

Once I was back in my office, I stared at the phone and wondered, *Should I give Ms. Jane a call or pay her a visit? I'm sure she won't change her mind. I can't deal with all this. Andreas, please can you come home? I don't want to go to the trial. Maybe there was a mistake like Marilyn suggested. Maybe Ms. Jane doesn't understand how important it is for me to be at the trial. Maybe she doesn't realize that this is the only way I can learn what happened to Andreas during the last moments of his life.*

Thinking Marilyn might be right, the next day I decided to reach out to Ms. Jane again. *I'll explain the importance of me being at the trial more clearly and ask her if she can come up with another solution.* Hopeful, I dialed her number.

"If we make an exception for you, then everybody else will want us to make an exception when something comes up for them." Ms. Jane's words barreled through the receiver and pierced my heart. I had always thought of her as a warm, caring administrator, but now I was unsure.

How can she place the brutality of murder on equal footing with illnesses and other family problems? How can an illness be equal to being beaten, butchered, and bludgeoned to death on the street with fists, a knife, and a wooden stick? If Andreas had been sick, at least we could've said goodbye. How can she be so by the book?

Later that day, driving home from school and still furious at Ms. Jane's bureaucratic response, I felt overcome with the rage that I was already carrying for what happened to Andreas. In addition to feeling a lack of compassion from my employer, I felt revictimized when the area's largest newspaper randomly and erroneously referred to my son as Juan Andreas Dresp. The reporter ended the story by raising suspicion and doubt, stating: ". . . not sure whether drugs were involved." *Is the implication that Andreas must've done something to deserve his violent death?* I wondered. Drugs weren't involved, but the newspaper never issued a correction, so in the archives, Andreas will forever remain Juan Andreas Dresp, a potential drug dealer or user.

This rage, in part, drove me to keep writing. I was compelled to give Andreas a voice, to tell people who he was in life—a loving, caring, intelligent, and thoughtful teenager with a bright future ahead of him—and what he suffered in death. I wanted to remind the world of who we had lost, how the life of my son was snuffed out by an act that took mere minutes. As a society, what responsibility do we have to address youth violence? At the local community level, shouldn't we be seeking out youths who are at risk of offending? Shouldn't we support, in every way possible, the victims of violent crime and their families?

That evening, I went to be with Andreas. I yearned to sit, if only for a few minutes, next to him before the night enveloped the cemetery in darkness.

Thursday, September 14, 1989
Dear Andreas,
I had a rough day at work because I received a response about my request for time off to attend the trial of the person accused of killing you. It wasn't what I'd hoped it would be. So here I am, just for a few minutes. It's almost seven thirty. The sun has just set, and the leaves of the trees surrounding your grave appear lifeless silhouetted against the indigo sky. Where are you, Andreas? I can't carry this pain anymore. I'm alone here in the cemetery except for the guard who's preparing to close the gates. It's time for me to leave.
Thinking of you every second of the day. I love you forever.
Mom
P.S. I will write to you again tomorrow.

Friday, September 15, 1989
Andreas,
It's very late, almost midnight, and I just now placed a bouquet of zinnias next to your pictures on the hutch. You smiled at me from the photo your friends took of you on that small boat in Maine. Remember that day? Knowing I will never see you smile again rips everything from me. My body feels hollow; only a

dark empty space remains. But aren't you coming back? Will I ever wake up from this nightmare?

The days are getting shorter, and a damp drizzle is mingling with a cool nip in the air. Autumn is fast-approaching, and Christmas will soon follow. It breaks my heart that you won't move forward with us through the coming seasons and years. Our family received the most extraordinary gift when you were born on January 24, 1970. You became part of the intimate fabric of our lives. Then you were gone, torn from us that summer night. Now all I have left are memories of your short life. You will forever remain in the summer of 1989.

Andreas, I miss having you nearby. I miss the simplest things like watching TV together, one show after another on a stormy winter's night. The fear of soon having to meet the person accused of causing your death weaves itself through my thoughts, into my dreams, and around my feelings.

I miss you with all my being. Every part of me hurts, still yearning for you.

Loving you always,

Mom

—༄—

Wednesday, September 20, 1989

Andreas,

Last Saturday evening, I went to see a movie with Julia. Being in the theater felt very strange to me, nothing like it used to feel. The excitement of waiting for the film to start was gone. I was more aware than usual of everybody around me. No matter where I looked, I saw young men and women—many about your age—hugging and laughing. Some of the couples held hands as they waited for the movie to start. Julia said to me with a quaver in her voice, "That's what you were robbed of . . . seeing Andreas grow into adulthood, being with a girl."

Julia also told me that she misses seeing you grow up. You know she loved you. "He was a very special child," she said. "From the moment I met him, I could tell he had a gentle spirit. He was so serene. He took life in stride."

I felt a little relief when the lights were turned down and I had to steer my attention toward the screen. But it was hard for me to get into the film. Thoughts of never seeing you grow up and never seeing you again kept haunting me.

Loving you always and thinking of you constantly, my dear son.

Mom

P.S. Fluff still misses you. She checks your room every morning, jumping up on your bed and rubbing the length of her long body against the headboard. In what has become a daily ritual, she kneads the stuffing of your pillows with her small paws until an indentation appears, then she turns her body around a few times, as if chasing her tail, before settling in at the head of your bed.

Thursday, September 21, 1989

Andreas, I'm sitting inside my car on the small path near your grave because it's raining today. Immense dark clouds rumble across a solid gray sky. Just now, I noticed an opening directly above the trees. Brilliant rays of sunshine, glistening golden threads, are streaming through the clouds and creating a heavenly glow. Is it you greeting me? Do you see me writing here next to your buried body?

My heart is breaking. I will love you forever my precious child.

Mom

—⚬—

Saturday, September 23, 1989

Andreas, I'm at your grave again and want to tell you about an experience I had while driving here today. Shortly before reaching the cemetery gate, I felt compelled to turn right onto a side street. I parked my car, crossed the street, and walked toward an old brick house covered with English ivy. I've walked by that house before and know that it's a place that offers family and couple's therapy. A sign on the lawn read, "Spiritual Psychotherapy Workshop."

A tall young man dressed in white stood at the front door. I stepped toward him as if an invisible force was guiding me into that building. He wore a gold necklace with an eagle pendant similar to yours. Smiling, he introduced himself as a psychologist and the leader of the workshop. Right away I felt at ease; it was like he'd been expecting me. Was that sense of ease coming from you, Andreas, telling me that the workshop had something to offer me?

Since your death, I've felt momentary sensations of warmth deep inside my heart. At times, when I close my eyes, I can even see a faint flickering flame struggling to come alive inside me.

Entering the large, dimly lit room, I lowered myself onto one of the floor cushions that had been arranged in a circle. Next to me, two women spoke quietly with their heads bent toward one another. More women and men took their seats until the leader joined the circle to introduce the workshop, which he explained would be about the spirit.

"How do we get in touch with that force? How do we invite it to become present in our psychotherapeutic encounters?" he asked rhetorically before instructing us to "go within" by closing our eyes. *Is that how we can see far into our innermost selves?*

I wondered. I sat cross-legged, as if in a yoga lotus pose. With my hands resting on my knees, I closed my eyes to shut out what little light was in the room. The psychologist's gentle guiding voice trailed off as my mind wandered back in time.

Andreas, in the depth of the darkness, sitting in a circle among strangers, I was transported to that terrible night. I could vividly see your friends Mike, Todd, and Sam standing with me in our kitchen after they'd run up the back stairs, their chests expanding rapidly, breathless and gasping for air as their hearts beat fast, when suddenly the shrill ring of our doorbell interrupted us. At the front door, I was stunned to see your friend Tim, accompanied by a young police officer, standing on the doorstep. Without a word, Tim slowly extended his arm toward me, and I saw that he was holding your worn leather wallet in his hand. I felt the brush of his hand as, eyes averted, he placed the wallet in my palm. He turned toward the officer who, standing just behind him, stepped forward and said, "Get to the hospital as quickly as possible."

"Keep breathing deeply," the psychologist's voice sounded far away and interrupted my vision, so I shifted my legs slightly on the floor cushion. "Please open your eyes gradually. Take your time," he said, drawing me back to the present. My right hand trembled against my leg, so I shifted my weight again.

I first opened my eyes just a slit. Through the haze, I could see men, women, and bare walls. "Come back into the room gradually," I heard the psychologist say softly. As I opened my eyes fully, Tim and the police officer disappeared, leaving me alone in a group of strangers, my legs trembling and my heart pounding. Over time, the other people in the room became clearer, and the psychologist's white shirt and gold necklace shined in front of me. "How did it feel?" he asked the group. "Does anybody want to share their experience?" Tears drenched my face.

Before leaving, the instructor asked about the reason for my tears. I managed to tell him what happened to you, and he gave me a bibliography of books about death and the spirit. Andreas, was that the reason you sent me there?

If it stops raining, tomorrow your dad and I will hike Mount Monadnock in New Hampshire.

Love you forever,

Mom

—⚏—

The trial was set to start September 28, not quite four weeks into the school year. As the mother of the victim, I knew it was my civic duty to support the hard work of the prosecutor by attending; it never crossed my mind not to. My family and I wanted the person who took Andreas from us to be held accountable, and as his mother, my need to be present and bear witness to my son's final hours—no matter how painful the details of those last hours might be—was profound.

As the trial date neared, my boss, Ms. Jane, came around and strongly supported my decision to attend the trial. She had recognized the importance of this and encouraged me to take as many days off as needed. Still, it had become clear to me that I would have to use all of my sick and personal days in order to attend. By then, I had already accepted the fact because I knew that during the school year, I would get some respite due to scheduled school vacations and holidays. I loved my job as a social worker and psychotherapist and was counting on that love to help me remain healthy, committed, and focused on my work.

On the day before the trial began, I wrote again to Andreas.

Wednesday, September 27, 1989

Dear Andreas,

I was just going to write, in a second of absentmindedness, "How are you?" But you, in your body, are no longer here. Your soul is. I have to believe that. You are still with me, that is, around or within me, or you are where souls go.

Andreas, tomorrow morning during the selection of the jury, we're going to see for the first time the one accused of killing you. As long as I don't let my thoughts wander, I can pretend that he has nothing to do with me. He is a stranger. I just happen to be in the courtroom observing a murder trial unfold—or maybe a play. If I let my mind go, I feel terribly scared. Images appear of all we have lost. Because of the murderer, you have no chance to grow up, become a man, and live your life. Because of him, we were robbed of seeing you smile as you receive your college diploma. We cannot celebrate your graduation. I miss you every moment of every day. Each moment I'm reminded of what will never be: Never again will Andreas . . . never again will he . . . Tom lost his precious and only brother, and now he must go on alone through this world. I could go on and on. You know how much you and all of us have lost.

Andreas, today I took out your gold chain with the eagle pendant, the one you bought with your hard-earned money. I wore it this morning together with the locket my friends gave me for my first birthday without you. It was four days after you were killed, and I turned forty-four. I intend to wear the eagle and the locket again tomorrow when the trial starts in the hope that they will give me strength through the invisible presence of you and my friends.

Andreas, tomorrow you will be with me in my heart every moment of the day.

Love,

Your aching mom

PART II

I tie your eagle necklace around my neck,
hoping that remnants of your sweat
mingle with mine.
I stare at your brother's earlobe,
remembering you.

I listen to your friends' stories,
cling to their words as a rock climber clings
to the edge of a mountain.
I replay the images of their stories
as often as I can, trying to bring you back.

I clutch each piece of your clothing,
the green shirt you wore, your gray jeans.
I hold your last pillowcase,
searching for strands of your brown hair,
for your smell.

Where are you!?
Where did you go?

CHAPTER 6

The Jury

On Thursday, September 28, the first day of the murder trial, Robert and I got up as usual, just like we had during the past few weeks to go to work. Since Tom was back in school, he decided not to attend the trial. In silence, Robert went to shower first. I tried to eat something to calm the rumbling in my stomach. As I took a bite of a buttered English muffin, I was reminded that this was Andreas's favorite food to eat before rushing out the door for school.

After Robert finished showering, he and I swapped places; he went into the kitchen, and I stepped into the bathroom to ready myself for our first encounter with the one accused of killing our son. *How do we dress to go to the trial of our son's accused murderer? If we put on the right clothes, will Andreas come back? Will the nightmare be over?* I knew that the best I could hope for was to find out exactly what had happened leading up to Andreas's death. *I'll just wear the gray pants and the green sweater I wear to work, nothing special, no dressing up.* Robert put on a light blue shirt, khaki pants, a navy-blue jacket, and a maroon tie, clothes he usually wore to the office. Once outside our house on that bright fall day, Robert looked as if only his familiar tie and buttoned-up jacket were holding him together. *Is he, too, close to collapsing?* I wondered. The way his black curly hair fell to his brow reminded me of Andreas.

Without uttering a word, Robert and I drove to the courthouse—a place I didn't want to go. Our neighborhood now felt foreign to me.

Just as my life had become unfamiliar in the wake of my son's death, the streets now appeared eerie, as if draped in fog.

What's it going to be like being part of a murder trial? Will I find out something I didn't know about Andreas? He was so sweet, so lovable. Did he have a hidden personality? It can't be. I knew my dear Andreas his entire life. Will the defense attorney make him look like a criminal so that the accused can walk free? I didn't know what was going through Robert's mind. The agony each of us carried in our own way had created distance between us. When I looked at Robert, I saw anguish, the same anguish I felt inside my own heart. I began to fear that if I said something to him, it would be the wrong thing. And I didn't want to cause either of us more pain.

After Robert and I passed through the metal detector at the entrance to the Massachusetts Superior Court building in Cambridge, we rushed through the crowded lobby toward the elevator. My breathing quickened as if we were racing up a mountain. We came to a standstill with a group of men and women who were also waiting for the elevator. As the squeaky doors slid open, we stepped into the dimly lit box, and the people around us followed. Robert pressed the button for the tenth floor, where Lucy's office was located. *Is one of these men the accused?* I felt my heart shudder in my chest. *Are these people members of his family?* I anxiously contemplated as the elevator labored to move upward.

Once we exited the elevator, I walked alongside Robert as he led us to Lucy's office. Robert was always good at finding his way. Even on that bright Sunday morning in June when Robert, Tom, and I left the hospital after having been told we had to leave Andreas "hooked up to the machines so the coroner can do his job," even then, Robert was able to find our car—the car that we'd parked when we were still a family of four.

When Robert knocked on Lucy's slightly open office door, she greeted us with an encouraging smile. The peace she exuded gave me a sense that we could cope with attending the trial as long as she was with us. Before going downstairs to the courtroom, she again calmly explained what we might expect. "They'll be selecting the jury this morning. The defendant will be present. It's his jury. They'll be the ones to decide his fate. You are allowed to sit in, but his lawyer *could* request that you not be present. The trial will most likely start today, after the jury is chosen."

When Lucy finished preparing us for what was to come next, Robert and I followed her into the empty elevator. As it haltingly descended, each floor brought me closer to the place where I would first lay eyes on the one accused of killing Andreas. As the elevator rattled to a stop at the sixth floor, where the courtrooms were located, I gasped for air.

The three of us stepped into a long corridor that was devoid of daylight and lined with closed wooden doors. Just outside the entrance to Courtroom B, Lucy asked Robert and me to stay there for a moment while she went to peek into the courtroom. A moment later, she returned and whispered, "The defendant is already seated. I'll walk you in."

"I'm staying here," I announced abruptly. "I'm not ready to go in."

"Take as much time as you need, Christine. I'll be right back," Lucy said before she led Robert into the courtroom.

I'm going to collapse when I see that monster. Do I really want to go in there?

A few minutes later, Lucy returned. "I'll wait here with you," she said calmly. "We have time. We can walk over to the door and just look into the courtroom to see how you feel."

After standing in the corridor for a while with Lucy by my side, I started to take slow steps toward the courtroom door. Once in front of it, I argued with myself internally, *Do I really want to see him? No, but I need to hear what happened to Andreas. I have to go in there.*

So as not to be seen, I leaned against the wall next to the courtroom entrance and looked over my shoulder through the glass-paneled door to catch a glimpse of the accused. Seeing only men and women in dark suits sitting behind large tables facing the judge, my head snapped back. *How strange . . . no monster.*

I turned to look again, this time more closely, and I noticed a significant age difference between the men at one table. Most of them looked close to my age—mid-forties or a bit younger—except one person who sat between two of the men in dark suits. He looked very young. As I focused on him, I noticed that he was white and resembled the teenager I'd seen on the front page of our newspaper some weeks earlier. He wore his short hair slicked back neatly; his black pin-striped suit jacket hung loosely over his narrow shoulders as if it belonged to an older relative or friend. *Oh my God! It's a child inside the suit.* I quickly twisted my body back to lean against the wall as my eyes welled with tears.

Images flashed through my mind of some of the young boys who attended the schools where I worked. I kept seeing a boy named Alex, who had a difficult time concentrating and often erupted in explosive, unpredictable outbursts that frightened his teachers. During my counseling sessions with Alex, he talked about the abuse he'd experienced at home and the violence he'd seen on the streets. He told me that even an intervention from the Department of Social Services hadn't stopped his father's rages. Like so many other children who didn't feel safe at home, Alex had no relatives nearby who could be there for him. Although he wanted to do well in school so that he could one day help his mother have a better life, he was often getting suspended.

As I wiped away my tears, Lucy slowly pulled open the squeaky-hinged door and followed me into the windowless courtroom. Filled with fear and trepidation, I wondered, *Is this where Andreas will be resurrected only to be taken from me again?* I was relieved when I spotted Robert, who had found us seats at the end of the second row from the front of the courtroom. Lucy and I quickly joined him. The row in front of us was empty, as front rows so often are at church services or community meetings. From our seats on the shellacked wooden bench that nearly spanned the width of the courtroom, we had a clear view of the proceedings.

Should I stay here? It's very crowded. I kept turning my head to see who was sitting behind me. *Who are all these men and women?* Lucy must have noticed my confusion because she whispered, "They're all part of the pool of potential jurors." Lucy explained that the jury pool consisted of between sixty to eighty people.

As artificial light from the large, round ceiling lamp illuminated the main characters like actors on a stage, my gaze turned to the young man who sat between the two attorneys at the table to my right. *Look away. Look at somebody else!* I pleaded with myself. *I don't want the image of the accused in my mind!* I forced my attention toward the raised platform at the front of the room where a black-robed man sat behind the judge's bench. I listened to every word he said. His thoughtful manner reassured me that he was in charge.

"Ladies and gentlemen, now the nature of the case is this: Mr. Corey McCale is accused of a murder said to have occurred on the night of June 10. The person said to have been murdered is Andreas Dresp. The offense is said to have occurred during a dispute between two groups of young people, after which, Mr. Dresp was found to have been stabbed and from the stab wound, he died.

"There are a couple of things I want you to keep in mind about our justice system," the judge continued matter-of-factly as he directed his attention toward the potential jurors seated in the gallery. "First, when a person is accused of a crime, he is presumed innocent until proven guilty. Second, it is the obligation of the prosecution to prove the defendant guilty. It is not up to the defense to prove him innocent. Furthermore, the prosecutor must prove that the defendant is guilty beyond a reasonable doubt, meaning that there is no other reasonable explanation based on the evidence presented.

"Now I will ask all of you potential jurors several questions," the judge said. "If you answer any one of these questions in the affirmative, please raise your hand."

The wooden bench beneath me felt cold and hard as I shifted slightly in my seat. I listened as the judge went through a series of questions and watched as the assembled panel of potential jurors thinned each time one of them responded to a question with a raised hand and was subsequently dismissed.

"I'm going to read off a list of names, and I want you to tell me, again by raising your hand, if you are acquainted with any of these people."

As he began to read aloud from a list of names unfamiliar to me, I wondered, *Is he presenting the characters that will be part of the play?* Suddenly, the resonant voice of the judge called out the names of my son and the accused. It seemed unnatural to hear their names together, side by side. The words jolted my body as if the judge, while forming them on his lips, had plugged them into a live wire connected to my body.

But no! This is not a play. A play would end. If this were a play, we'd be going back at the end of the day to our unchanged family. But this trial is real! Robert and I aren't impartial observers; whatever we hear will deeply impact us and our family and friends. Every day of the trial, we'll go home to our forever changed lives.

When the judge was finished with his questions, he addressed the remaining men and women in the jury pool. "Now, ladies and gentlemen, we're going to impanel a jury. Mr. Perez, the bailiff, will call your name and number. Once he does, please step over here to the jury box."

Dressed in a beige uniform with an official-looking badge pinned over the pocket of his crisp white dress shirt, Mr. Perez stood tall in front of the defendant's table. The bailiff's deep voice reverberated throughout the courtroom as he spoke directly to the defendant, "Will the defendant please rise? Corey McCale, you are now placed at the bar for trial. These good people whom I shall call are to pass judgment between the Commonwealth and you upon your trial. If you object to any one of them, you will do so through your counsel as their names are called and before they are sworn in. You may make an unlimited number of challenges for cause. You also have the right to make up to sixteen peremptory challenges, as limited by state statute, without providing a reason to the court. Please be seated."

One by one, the serious-looking, neatly dressed men and women in the jury pool were called from their seats in the gallery to the jury box near where the defendant sat. As the questioning got underway, some remained in the box while others were dismissed and instructed to leave. *What a strange game of chess.* I had never seen anything like it before. *What decisions are they making? How do they decide who will remain to become a juror and who goes home?* As this back-and-forth went on for some time, the pool of potential jurors eventually shrank.

Seeing the confused look on my face, Lucy whispered, "The technical term for what's going on is *challenging.* There are two ways the defendant and his lawyers can challenge the fitness of a potential juror to serve. The first is to challenge for cause—that's a request to remove a potential juror when there is reason to believe the person won't be able to serve impartially. The second way to remove someone from the jury pool is a peremptory challenge. This means that the defendant and his lawyers don't have to give a reason for their objection to a proposed juror. The defense can make as many challenges for cause as they want to, but only up to sixteen peremptory challenges."

I nodded my head as if I understood Lucy's explanation, but inside I was thinking, *Nothing makes sense to me. I feel like I've once again arrived in a new country. I'm watching people interact, but I have no clue what they're doing or why.* Luckily, the lawyers did seem to know what was going on. Their focused faces looked like they were playing a competitive game of chess, always thinking about their next move. *Could it be that if the defense attorney chooses the right jurors, it'll be easier for him to win the case? Who is the right juror? How strange to put so much effort and time into this process. Why do we need such a time-consuming and expensive procedure to put somebody in jail?*

A few moments later, Lucy quietly explained, "What's at work here is the defendant's right of being innocent until proven guilty. The lawyers on both sides know what kind of juror they're looking for to get the desired outcome."

What if the defense attorney gets his jurors, the ones he hopes won't have the courage to convict the defendant to life in prison because of his age? What if he walks out a free man? Does the legal system really work to protect victims of violent crimes? How can justice prevail in this huge legal bureaucracy—one in which the victim or the victim's family doesn't even get to choose their own lawyer? Despite the concerning questions racing through my mind, I felt some reassurance knowing that the Commonwealth represented Andreas.

Finally, the exchange of women and men in the jury box came to an end; the sixteen remaining in the box would make up the jury and its alternates. I maneuvered my gaze around the defendant in my continued attempt to avoid looking at him; seeing the men and women in the box stirred gratitude in my heart. *They are willing to hear every detail about what happened to Andreas, and they don't even know us. They'll witness his death and will be with me as I find out what happened to my son.*

For a moment, as the judge rose from the bench at the front of the room, smoothing the folds of his robe with opened palms, I saw someone else. He reminded me of the kind Lutheran pastor at the church I had attended during my teenage years at boarding school in Pforzheim, Germany. The memory, though fleeting, was a comfort, but as the judge spoke, I was brought back to the tension in the courtroom.

"First, you'll be sworn in as jurors," the judge announced.

When all sixteen jurors solemnly raised their right hands, I realized that the trial would begin soon. I felt Robert shift in his seat next to me as the judge continued with instructions to the jurors.

"Of the sixteen of you, four will be alternates. But we won't decide which of you are alternates until the end of the trial, so it doesn't make any difference in what order you were picked or what seat you're in, you're all members of the jury. A jury also has a foreperson. You will select your own foreperson at the end of the trial. The foreperson presides over jury deliberations, signs the verdict slip, and announces the verdict in open court. But apart from that, the foreperson is the same as the rest of the jurors." Finished with his instructions, the judge returned to his seat behind the bench, and a quiet stillness fell over the room.

Suddenly, the bailiff's voice cut through the silence, "All rise!" Everyone in the courtroom stood as the judge rose from his seat and exited the courtroom ahead of the jurors, who stepped out of their box in a single-file line. *What a somber sight. It took just minutes to transform regular-looking men and women into people who hold justice in their hands. Like me, they will sit in this room and hear the evidence. Like me, they will surely be impacted by what they see and hear. As jurors, they will carry the weight of whatever their verdict is. This experience and their decisions will impact them—like me, like all of us in this room—for the rest of their lives.* Without a sound, the attorneys who'd been seated at the front tables followed the jurors and the judge out of the room. Our friends, the parents of some of Andreas's friends, and Robert and I stood with Lucy waiting for the defendant's side to leave. Lucy kept her head high, scanning the surroundings. Once she saw that the defendant's family and friends had left the courtroom, she motioned for us to follow her into the hallway where we could take a short break before the start of the trial.

CHAPTER 7

Day One

After jury selection, Robert and I went to a quiet area of the corridor, away from the defendant's group. I began to pace in silence, slowly, back and forth, sensing only the rapid beating of my heart. Suddenly, my attention shifted when, out of the corner of my eye, I noticed a petite dark-haired woman in a lime-green suit marching toward me, her high heels clicking on the concrete floor. She stopped abruptly in front of me, her body rigid and her tense, narrow face capped by a fringe of short black curls. "Are you Andreas's mother?" she asked frankly.

"Yes," I replied, a bit taken aback. But my heart jumped, delighted that she'd said, "*Are* you," rather than "*Were* you." *I knew it! Andreas is alive! How normal and familiar it feels to hear his name spoken in the present tense.*

"I'm so sorry about what happened to your son." Her teary eyes met mine, and we briefly embraced. "It could've been my son. I've had nothing but trouble with him. I hope this opens his eyes, and he'll straighten himself out. He's not here right now, but when he comes, I want him to meet you."

As the stranger disappeared into the crowd on the other side of the corridor, Lucy informed me, "She's the mother of one of the defendant's friends. Her son will be called to testify."

A little weight lifted off my body because, in her, I recognized my own difficulties as a mother with no extended family nearby raising two sons in a complex society that worships violence. *If the judge and the prosecutor do their work well, will Andreas be resting on his bed when we return home?*

After the short break, Lucy escorted Robert and me back into the nearly empty courtroom, and we returned to our seats on the long bench. The parents of some of Andreas's friends sat behind us, as they would do throughout the trial.

I spotted Djano, one of Andreas's close friends from high school who had always worn a friendly smile, sitting solemnly in the last row of the gallery. Though he had not been present on that Saturday night when Andreas was stabbed and beaten, I knew his attendance at the trial was born of a need to find out what had happened to his friend. The sight of him immediately brought back a memory of the celebration we had hosted in our backyard when Andreas and Djano had graduated from high school. I could still see Djano's Armenian mother walking across our lawn carrying a large tray of delicious homemade baklava, a special family recipe. None of us could have known then that violence would upend our lives and take Andreas's life just one year later.

I sat between Robert and Lucy. *Is this the way for us to be present with Andreas on the last night of his life?* I thought as my body became heavier. *Andreas, this time your dad and I will be with you.* My gaze followed the movement of the actors in dark suits as they came onto the stage. The attorneys carried folders and boxes and placed them on the large tables. Mr. Rapacki and his co-counsel, Ms. Sanchez, each put a folder next to their chairs. As if they really were on a theater stage, bright lights shined upon them, which made it possible for me to notice how calm and secure they acted as they prepared for the opening of the trial.

While waiting, I caught myself glancing to my right, past Lucy, to where the mother of the defendant was taking her seat. I was curious to see what she looked like. She wore a gray dress the color of storm clouds. Curly brown hair framed her pale, blank face. It was hard not to wonder what she was feeling, how she was coping. As a mother of two boys myself and as a social worker who worked to help parents and children deal with life's difficulties, I'd stood with the mothers of young boys who'd been summoned to juvenile court. Though accustomed to putting myself in another mother's place, I was surprised to feel a moment of calm when I saw her surrounded by a group of women who I presumed to be her family and friends.

When the bailiff ordered, "All rise," everyone in the courtroom sprang up in unison like soldiers at attention. With their heads bowed, as if dragging heavy weights around their shoulders, the jurors entered. The judge soon followed, taking his place at the desk behind the bench. "Everyone, please be seated," he said.

"Please stand," Mr. Perez directed the defendant whose two lawyers stood next to him. "Members of the jury, Corey McCale, the defendant, is charged with murdering Andreas Dresp."

Hearing Andreas's name so close to the word *murder* made the tips of my fingers turn ice-cold.

"With regards to this indictment," Mr. Perez continued, "the defendant has pleaded not guilty. You are now sworn to try the issues. If he is guilty, you are to say so; if he is not guilty, you are to say so and no more."

—∿—

For a moment, I was able to ignore everyone on the stage except Mr. Rapacki. He stepped toward a small podium and placed some sheets of paper on it. Grasping the podium's varnished wooden edges, he lifted his head, glanced at the audience, then faced the jurors. "My name is Ed Rapacki, and I'm an assistant district attorney here in Middlesex County. Sitting with me at the counsel table is Ms. Sanchez. She's also an assistant district attorney. Together, we have the privilege of representing the Commonwealth of Massachusetts during this trial."

Is he going to be able to say what he needs to say? Will I be able to endure his words?

"The Commonwealth has an obligation, and the obligation is to prove to each one of you beyond a reasonable doubt that the defendant, Corey McCale, murdered Andreas Dresp. Throughout the trial, you will see Mr. McCale present; you will not see Andreas Dresp. At the time of his death, Andreas was nineteen years old. He lived in Belmont with his parents and older brother, and he'd just finished his first year of college. On the night of Saturday, June 10 of this year, he went with some friends to a carnival in Belmont."

Andreas lives! Mr. Rapacki is talking about our son and his friends at the local carnival. What a relief! But why is he talking about him in the past tense? What are words of death and murder doing alongside Andreas's name?

I didn't want to miss hearing anything that related to Andreas's fate. Intellectually, I knew he was dead and had been murdered. But on an emotional level, a part of me felt that he was still alive. I could see him in his gray jeans and freshly ironed green-striped shirt, his gold necklace with the eagle pendant hanging from his neck. *Didn't Andreas just ask me, "Mom, which shirt should I wear, the green one or the blue one? Which looks better on me?"*

Mr. Rapacki's words began to paint scenes from the last night of Andreas's life. "At the carnival," he said, "Andreas and his friends met two young women who invited them to go to Glacken Field, which is next to the Fresh Pond Golf Course in Cambridge, just a few blocks from where the victim lived with his family in Belmont. It was there, at Glacken Field, that Andreas Dresp and his friends from Belmont first encountered a group of youths from Cambridge."

Mr. Rapacki went on to describe the similarly aged young men from the neighboring town who'd also gone out that night. That group had met at a basketball court in Cambridge and drank a few beers while they played ball before deciding to head over to Harvard Square, closer to Belmont. "There wasn't much happening at the Square, so they moved on to visit the home of a friend, Zach Doxon, who you will hear more about later," I heard Mr. Rapacki say.

"When Andreas and his friends arrived at Glacken Field, there were a few Cambridge kids in the parking lot and others sitting on the nearby bleachers. Not knowing any of these people, Andreas and his friends felt uncomfortable and decided to leave. But as they walked toward their car, which was parked at the golf course, they encountered two individuals from Cambridge," the prosecutor continued. "Andreas's friend Tim Killilea looked at the Cambridge kids as he passed them, and one of them, Jarod Lodish, asked, 'What are you staring at?' Tim Killilea replied, 'Who's staring?' As words were exchanged, the situation escalated quickly when Jarod Lodish retrieved a baseball bat from the trunk of his nearby car and threatened Andreas Dresp, Tim Killilea, and their friends with it."

Andreas is still alive! He's with his friends!

I thought of a conversation I'd had with Brian Walsh, one of Andreas's friends, a few weeks after Andreas was killed. "Later that night, we went to Glacken Field with Mike to meet up with a girl he'd met at the carnival," Brian had recounted. "This girl, her name is Amy, told Mike there was a party at the field. When we got there, we were surprised to see Amy and her friends were already there with some other guys. Still, they seemed okay. We were all talkin' and stuff. It wasn't until a different group of guys showed up that things began to get uncomfortable. One of these new guys asked, 'Do you have a pass?' and Tim answered, 'No, we don't need a pass. This is a free country.' The guy didn't like Tim's answer, so he threatened to beat us with a baseball bat. Tim told him, 'If you're gonna fight, fight clean.' We didn't know what kind of kids we were dealin' with. We were stupid."

The sound of Mr. Rapacki's strong and clear voice pulled me back to reality. "During this encounter, someone whistled loudly to signal more young men from the Cambridge group to come running down the bleachers toward the victim and his friends. It was at this point that Andreas Dresp and his friends jumped into their vehicle and began to drive away, chased on foot by the Cambridge crowd.

"It should've ended there—we all wish it had ended there—but it didn't. Instead, fueled by youthful impulsivity, anger, and alcohol, the two groups met up again a short while later at the intersection of Grove Street and Huron Avenue in Cambridge, right at the Belmont town line—but not before getting additional recruits and arming themselves.

"Now, Andreas lived just two blocks away, so he and a couple of his friends did a very stupid thing: They went to his nearby home and took a broomstick and two cutoff hockey sticks from the family garage. As they were retrieving these items, some of their other friends went to another house in Belmont, where there was a party going on, and gathered reinforcements, telling partygoers that they had just been chased and threatened by a bunch of kids from Cambridge and needed help."

The prosecutor's words caused my body to shudder. *Our sweet son and his close friends were going to fight?* I couldn't fit that notion into my view of Andreas and his friends. *Them in a fight? Please, Mr. Rapacki, this can't be. Andreas has never been in a fight!*

"And so, three or four carloads of kids from Belmont drove to the intersection of Huron and Grove. They parked their cars on the street and followed a path that led them to the golf course's parking lot. Several of the kids from Belmont had broomsticks or hockey sticks, and one or two grabbed tree branches. As they came up the steps, they encountered three or four stragglers from the Cambridge group. When one of the Belmont kids asked, 'Do you want to fight now?' the Cambridge kids answered, 'No! We weren't the ones giving you a hard time.' When one of Andreas's friends realized he recognized one of these kids as an acquaintance, that was enough to diffuse the situation, at least for the time being.

"And so, the two groups dispersed. The reason they split up was because a police cruiser came into the parking lot. The kids from Belmont backed down to the golf course and took the path to retrace their steps back to their cars. When they got to the street, they saw a police cruiser, so they stepped back onto the path, which gave them some cover, and waited for the cruiser to pass by.

"Soon there were fifteen to twenty kids from Belmont gathered at the intersection. As two of them headed to their cars, they noticed four people walking down Huron Avenue. Two of the four were opening the doors to the Belmont kids' cars, looking in and then shutting the doors as they moved on.

"As the Cambridge kids walked further down Huron Avenue away from Belmont, a couple of the Belmont kids stood in the street and yelled, 'Where are you now? Where's everybody for the fight?'

"Just then, a car came around the corner, picked up the four individuals from Cambridge who'd been looking inside the Belmont kids' cars, and drove to an area called Corcoran Park, which is a residential area across from Belmont Cemetery, just south of the intersection of Huron and Grove. And there the kids from Cambridge did a very stupid thing: They went to a party at the home of Zach Doxon and told the partygoers, 'There's a bunch of people from Belmont with sticks challenging us to a fight.' And so, twenty-five to thirty kids from Cambridge picked up sticks and started running to the intersection.

"But they didn't just pick up sticks, ladies and gentlemen, because just prior to leaving Zach Doxon's house, the defendant, Corey McCale, opened a drawer in the kitchen, saw some knives, and asked Zach if he could take some of them. When Zach said yes, the defendant took a large kitchen knife for himself and handed another one to his close friend Kevin Smith. On his way out, Mr. Smith was drinking a Beck's beer, carrying a broomstick, and holding the knife that Mr. McCale had given him. Armed with his own pocketknife, Mr. Doxon and his friends headed to the intersection in search of the kids from Belmont."

Mr. Rapacki continued to set the scene for the jurors as the entire courtroom listened intently. "They cut through a residential area and came out onto Huron Avenue, about two hundred yards from the intersection with Grove Street," he said. "Some of them were running as they moved toward the intersection, and when a police cruiser approached them from behind, somebody yelled, 'Cruiser!' At that point, Kevin Smith tossed his knife, his beer bottle, and his broomstick alongside Huron Avenue, then walked to the intersection. The police cruiser continued down Huron, turned right onto Grove, and headed north. Moments later, the kids from Belmont and the kids from Cambridge finally collided at Huron and Grove. Standing ten to fifteen feet apart, one individual from the Cambridge group walked up to Randy Harvey, one of the boys from Belmont, and gave him a sucker punch—meaning he hit him from the side when he wasn't looking—and knocked him down. The punch was so loud that everybody could hear it, and that's when all hell broke loose.

"You will hear testimony from Kevin Smith, who became engaged in a fight with the victim at that moment. They first exchanged blows and then started to wrestle."

I watched Mr. Rapacki's lips as he formed the words that made everybody around me disappear. *I feel like I'm witnessing the attack, but I can't do anything to intervene. Must I sit here, nailed to this bench, and watch as Andreas moves toward death? Please, Mr. Rapacki, don't let me hear that my nineteen-year-old son punched and was punched in return. Please say the cruisers stopped, turned on their flashing lights, and called for backup. Please say they warned the crowd with their loudspeakers that they would be arrested. Please don't let the officer drive away from the crowd, please, please!*

"Within a minute or two, several police cruisers arrived on the scene. But before they did, individuals had paired off, some fought, some didn't. Kevin Smith and Andreas Dresp punched each other and wrestled their way down Huron, away from where the others were fighting."

Please let me be there to stop the attack. Please let me soothe Andreas's pain. What worthless hands of mine! What good are they if they can't even comfort my frightened son? What good am I if I can't give up my life for him?

With the volume of his voice rising slightly, as if imparting his words with the full weight of their meaning, Mr. Rapacki painted bloodier images with each word he spoke. "And as they were wrestling, the defendant, Corey McCale, came from behind and to the side of Andreas Dresp with a kitchen knife that measured eleven and a half inches and had a six-and-five-eighths-inch blade and plunged it into Andreas's side, between two ribs. Mr. McCale didn't stop until the handle had met the skin. In pulling out the knife, the handle broke off from the blade. Still wrestling with Andreas, Kevin Smith saw the defendant and said, 'Corey, get his hands! Get his hands!' Instead, the defendant punched Andreas Dresp in the face several times.

"The defendant then picked up a stick and went . . . ," Mr. Rapacki raised his hand above his head to demonstrate how Corey McCale had struck Andreas in the head with the stick, "*whomp.* After that, Andreas finally let go of Mr. Smith." The sound of Mr. Rapacki's ghastly words filled the hushed courtroom.

Where am I? Was this just done to my son? Am I with him just observing? Why can't I intervene? Why can't I move to throw myself between Andreas and the stick? What kind of mother am I if I can't protect my son?

"Then," Mr. Rapacki said, speaking directly to the jury, "Kevin Smith and Corey McCale left Andreas Dresp bleeding in the street. As they ran from the scene with the defendant still clutching the stick he'd used to bludgeon the victim, a police officer shouted, 'Drop the stick!' It was then that Kevin Smith saw Corey McCale toss the stick off to the side of the road. At that point, Smith and McCale split up and managed to evade the police.

"After returning to Zach Doxon's apartment, the defendant told Mr. Doxon and Mr. Smith that he'd stabbed somebody. He also demonstrated how he'd stabbed the victim. But you won't hear any-body say that they *witnessed* the defendant stab Andreas Dresp because nobody saw it.

"While the defendant was back at the apartment in Cambridge, drinking alcohol with his friends, Andreas Dresp was rushed to the hospital, where medical staff worked frantically to save his life. But nine hours later, Andreas Dresp was dead after surgery failed to repair the extensive damage the stab wound had inflicted upon his liver."

Has everybody stopped breathing? Are people still around me? I know my body is on the courtroom bench between Robert and Lucy, but was I not just with Andreas on the street where he was stabbed? His beauti-ful face punched, and his head hit with a stick? The blood Mr. Rapacki referred to was my son's blood, my blood, my family's blood. It flowed down Huron Avenue, just a short block from the Grove Street Play-ground where, years earlier as a young mother, I had joyfully watched Andreas take his first steps as his spirited older brother, Tom, looked on with delight. Andreas's dark brown eyes were full of wonder then as he sat in the sandbox, letting the gritty, sun-soaked grains flow through his tiny hands, repeatedly turning them into a funnel.

Standing tall, shoulders squared toward the jury box, Mr. Rapacki continued, "The following day, after hearing from Kevin Smith that Andreas had died, the defendant went back to the scene of the fight, telling Zach Doxon that he remembered the handle had broken off from the blade. But the handle couldn't be found because the police had already located and retrieved it the night before. Realizing this, the defendant asked another friend, Ian Pooler, 'Do you think they can get fingerprints off the bloody handle of a knife?'

"Over the next three days, the defendant talked to his friend Kevin Smith about the stabbing, about not telling anybody, and about the need to keep the information to themselves. 'Don't mention it over the phone,' Corey McCale told his friend. Fortunately, the police were diligently working the investigation. In addition to finding the murder weapon in a pool of blood—with the handle of the knife separated from the blade—they also found some other knives alongside Huron Avenue, including a kitchen knife next to a Beck's beer bottle about four hundred feet away from where the stabbing occurred.

"The importance of these details will be made clear throughout this trial," stated the prosecutor. "You will hear from a fingerprint analyst and other experts. You'll learn that the only person who could possibly be responsible for the death of Andreas Dresp is the defendant, Corey McCale. You'll also hear testimony from Andreas's friends and those of the defendant, all who participated in the fight. The scientific evidence, in and of itself, will not prove to you beyond a reasonable doubt that Corey McCale murdered Andreas Dresp, but the testimony of the witnesses will—specifically, the testimony of Kevin Smith, Zach Doxon, and others whom the defendant confessed to.

"At the conclusion of the case, when I stand before you again, I will repeat what I'm about to tell you now: If you listen to all the evidence and apply to that evidence your own common sense and the law, as His Honor will instruct you to do, you will come to the only reasonable, rational conclusion: that eighteen-year-old Corey McCale is guilty of the murder of Andreas Dresp."

Having finished his opening argument, Mr. Rapacki went back to his seat just as calmly as he'd walked to the podium. I could see the mother of the accused out of the corner of my right eye. *Does she also feel nailed to the bench but for a different reason than I do?* I wondered.

Mr. Harris, the short, heavyset defense attorney, was up next. He walked to the podium with quick steps, briefly introduced himself and his co-counsel, Mr. Kohl, and addressed the jury. His acerbic tone of voice made it clear that his goal was to instill doubt in the prosecutor's opening argument. "What I say is not evidence," he began, "and what Mr. Rapacki just told you, that's not evidence. Now, members of the jury, as you sit here and listen to the answers that Kevin Smith will give in response to the prosecutor's questions, really listen to him when he tells you that on a different day, at a different place, he told a different story. Hear his motivation . . . his bias." It was obvious the defense attorney was implying that the witness, the defendant's close friend, had changed his story at least once. I was glad he didn't stay at the podium for long.

Standing to face the jurors, the judge began to speak, "Ladies and gentlemen of the jury, I'll now explain what the prosecution is required to prove and the degree to which it is required to prove it. Remember that the burden of proof falls on the prosecution, and the defendant is presumed innocent until proven guilty beyond a reasonable doubt. At the end of the trial, your task is to decide whether the prosecution has proved beyond a reasonable doubt that the defendant is guilty of the murder of Andreas Dresp. Reasonable doubt means that after careful consideration and comparison of all the evidence, you as a jury cannot say with moral certainty that he is guilty of the charges leveled against him."

Will this legal system work? I contemplated. *Wasn't the defendant offered a plea bargain, which means he would've had to admit his guilt?*

"In this case, the defendant is accused of murder, which is defined as an act committed with intent to injure or kill that leads to the death of another person. It's up to the jury to decide whether it was murder in the first degree or murder in the second degree. For murder in the second degree, the prosecution must prove that the stabbing of Andreas Dresp was committed to kill or inflict serious bodily injury. For murder in the first degree, the prosecution must also prove that the killing was deliberately premeditated."

Following the judge's explanation to the jury, he and the lawyers chatted at the sidebar, their faces serious under the artificial light. Shortly thereafter, the lawyers returned to their respective tables as a weighty silence once again fell upon the room.

"Mr. Rapacki, call your first witness, please," the judge instructed.

"Your Honor, the Commonwealth calls Robert Dresp," Mr. Rapacki said.

As Robert rose from his seat, he glanced at me and Lucy before moving toward the witness stand. Even though I knew that he would be the one to introduce Andreas to the jury, I couldn't believe what I was seeing: Robert a witness in a murder trial! He looked like a different man than he had just a few months ago. His formerly straight, five-foot, nine-inch frame appeared to be bent beneath the weight of loss. *Why is he going up to the witness stand? Mr. Rapacki referred to him as the first witness. What has he witnessed? Where am I? Why is Robert standing in the witness box lifting his right hand?*

My role at the trial was to be present each day and sit in the second row of the gallery so that the jurors could see the mother of the invisible, yet ever-present, victim of the crime. Robert had the same role as well as the small introductory part in which he was to characterize Andreas as our son and Tom's brother. *Don't the two of us have another purpose for being here? Isn't our presence in the courtroom also a way to be with Andreas during the last moments of his life, to bear witness to his execution on the street with a knife and stick? Isn't this a way for us to see how hanging out with his friends a few blocks from our house became a crime for Andreas that carried an instant death penalty?*

"Sir, in a loud, clear voice, please state your full name and spell your last name," Mr. Rapacki's voice interrupted my thoughts.

"My name is Robert Dresp. D-R-E-S-P."

"And please tell the court where you live."

"I live in Belmont," Robert answered.

"Who do you live there with?"

From the witness stand, Robert answered slowly, "My son, Tom, and my wife, Christine."

Why didn't he include Andreas?

"Do you have another son?"

"Not anymore," Robert's voice trembled.

Of course we do!

"What was his name?"

"Andreas."

"How old was Andreas and when was he born?"

"He was nineteen. He was born January 24, 1970."

"Did he go to school?"

"Yes. He'd just finished his freshman year of college at the University of Massachusetts in Lowell."

"Mr. Dresp, can you tell the jurors how tall Andreas was and how much he weighed?"

"He was six feet two and weighed approximately 190 pounds."

How can Andreas be in our past, Robert? I cried out internally. *Is he not still our son? Are we not still his parents?*

When Mr. Rapacki motioned for Robert to go to the easel, he stepped out of the witness stand, walked past the lawyers and the accused, and stopped in front of the jury. Then Mr. Rapacki handed Robert a long pointer and asked him to locate on the map our house, the playground next to it, and the place across the street where Andreas was killed. Robert did as instructed, although his hand was unsteady as if the pointer were too heavy to hold. To me, Robert seemed different than the way I'd often imagined he'd be at work, pointing to important information on the board with a sureness of being. His oval face—the same face that three months earlier still had a smile like Andreas's—appeared contorted.

After Robert returned to the witness stand, Mr. Rapacki continued questioning him. "Mr. Dresp, in the early evening hours of June 10, did you see your son Andreas?"

"Yes, I saw him around six o'clock that evening."

"And what was he doing when you saw him?"

"He was getting ready to go out with his friends."

"And did you see your son leave?"

"I don't remember seeing him leave, but I saw him getting dressed and getting ready to leave."

"And have you seen your son since, sir?"

"Not alive."

"Your Honor, I have no further questions for Mr. Dresp at this time."

"Mr. Harris, do you wish to cross-examine this witness?"

"No, Your Honor," the defense attorney replied.

"Thank you, sir. You may step down," the judge said to Robert.

Robert returned to the wooden bench to sit next to me in silence.

"Mr. Rapacki, your next witness, please," the judge requested.

"Your Honor, the Commonwealth calls Mr. Todd Giles."

Todd is here? If Todd is here, Andreas must be here as well. When Todd entered the courtroom, I couldn't help but think, *Oh my God, he looks so much older.* He looked fragile, as if it were taking great effort to hold his slender body erect.

After taking the oath to testify truthfully before the court, Todd took his seat in the witness box.

Todd being sworn in at a murder trial? How strange.

"How old are you, Mr. Giles?"

"Nineteen."

"Do you go to school, sir?"

"Yes, I'm a sophomore in college."

"Mr. Giles, did you know Andreas Dresp?"

"Yes."

"How did you know him?"

"He was my best friend."

"Mr. Giles, thinking back to June 10, did you spend any time with Mr. Dresp that day?"

"Yes. I spent the whole day with him. I was in his room at his house. He was makin' a music tape for me."

"Mr. Giles, could you speak louder for the jurors?"

"Alright."

"At some point, did you leave Andreas's house?"

"Yeah. I went home to go eat."

"And what time was that?"

"Around six o'clock."

"Did you see Andreas later that evening?"

"Yes. We went to a party."

"Just the two of you, or were there other people with you?"

"It was Andreas, Mike, Tim, me, Eric, and Jeff."

"What time did you go to the party?"

"We left for the party, I'd say, around eight o'clock."

"How long were you at the party?"

"About two hours."

"Did you consume any alcoholic beverages at the party?"

"Yes."

"How many?"

"About three or four beers."

"Did you happen to notice whether or not Andreas consumed any alcoholic beverages?"

"Yes, he did."

"What did he drink?"

"Beer."

"And you left the party at what time?"

"It was prob'ly around ten thirty or eleven o'clock."

"Where did you go?"

"We went to the carnival in Belmont."

"How long were you at the carnival?"

"Maybe forty-five minutes."

"Did you meet anybody there?"

"Yes, Mike met a girl named Amy."

"And what happened after Mike met Amy?"

"We were all hangin' around outside the carnival, so she told us to come to a party at the parking lot of Fresh Pond Golf Course. About half an hour later, we headed over to the parking lot where the party was supposed to be."

"What time was it then?"

"Eleven thirty, maybe."

"And where did you go?"

"To the parking lot near the main entrance of Fresh Pond Golf Course. I'm not sure of the name, but there's also a field and basketball courts there."

"Would that be Glacken Field?"

"Yes, sir. That's it."

"And you parked where?"

"We parked right in the parking lot."

"And what happened after you parked in the parking lot?"

"We went over to some bleachers where they all were, and the six of us—that'd be me, Andreas, Tim, Mike, Jeff, and Eric—sat separately. Then some Cambridge kids—I assumed they were from Cambridge— were sayin', 'Where's your guest passes?'"

"Objection, Your Honor!" Mr. Harris interrupted.

"Overruled," the judge said dismissively. Then turning to Todd, he said, "Mr. Giles, you may continue."

"We just sat there by ourselves. Some of the people were nice— they were comin' up and introducin' themselves to us—but we decided to leave 'cause we felt there was some tension."

"Objection, Your Honor! Hearsay!" Mr. Harris exclaimed.

"Overruled."

"How long were you at the bleachers?" Mr. Rapacki continued.

"About twenty minutes."

"And where did you go after you decided to leave?"

"We went back to the parking lot, but there were some guys there and one of them had a baseball bat. He was swingin' it and sayin' stuff, and our friend Tim started sayin' stuff back."

Andreas, please come home right now, I begged. *Don't stay at the park. I'm waiting for you at home.*

"And what happened after that?" Mr. Rapacki questioned.

"We went back to Andreas's house and grabbed some sticks."

"Now, Mr. Giles, when you say 'sticks,' do you mean tree branches?"

"No. They were hockey sticks."

"And where did you go after leaving Andreas's house?"

"We walked through the Grove Street Playground back toward the golf course."

"Can you tell me where the playground is on this map?"

"Yes, it's the area marked in blue. It's right behind Andreas's house."

"Thank you. And did you take the sticks with you?"

"We did, but then we hid them in the playground."

"So you didn't take them with you to the golf course?"

"No. We did not."

"What happened next?"

"We stopped on the pathway by a house near the golf course and talked about it. We realized that if there was a fight, we'd be outnumbered, so it was decided that Mike, Jeff, Eric, and I would go to another friend's house in Belmont, where there was a party, to get more people."

It can't be. I can't believe Andreas and his friends would make such a decision. I can't believe Andreas would get into a fight! What's happening? Did I not even know my own son? He's never been in a fight! He loved being with his friends. He was their peacekeeper. He was always stepping in when emotions heated up. Please, can one of you say you don't need to get more guys. Please, one of you say: 'Come on, let's get away from here. We don't need any trouble.' Can one of you please say it?

"Mr. Giles, when you returned from the party with more people, what happened next?" Mr. Rapacki asked.

"We went back to the place where we'd left Andreas and Tim."

"And were they still there?"

"Yes."

"What did you do once you found them?"

"We started walkin' through the golf course toward the parking lot."

"When you got to the parking lot, was there anyone there?"

"Yes, there were about six or seven Cambridge kids near the club-house. As far as I could tell, they were from Cambridge."

"Did you fight with them?"

"No."

"Why not?"

"The police came, so we all ran away."

"And did you or any of your friends have weapons at the time?"

"I didn't, but a couple did. Maybe three guys, I think."

"And what were these weapons."

"Cutoff hockey sticks and broomsticks."

"Mr. Giles, after you guys confronted the individuals from Cambridge near the clubhouse and you ran, you said that you walked back down when the police came. Where did you go?"

"We sat near the entrance goin' into the field; we sat at the bottom of the path that leads into the golf course."

"The area marked in orange on the map?"

"Right."

"And what did you do there?"

"Well, most of us stayed there, and then Brian, and I think Ben, walked up to the street where they saw some Cambridge kids breakin' into our friend Scott's car."

"Now, when you say Brian and Ben, who are they?"

"They were at the party in Belmont then came back with us."

"And what did you observe at that point?"

"I think it was Brian who started yellin', 'They're comin' back,' so we all ran up toward Huron Avenue. There was a white car with some kids gettin' out of it, but when we got to the street, they got back in the car and left."

"And then what did you do?"

"We stayed there for prob'ly about five minutes. I think most of us just assumed it was all over, so Tim, Andreas, and our friend Sam started to leave. And the next thing we knew, we saw the Cambridge kids comin' back down Huron."

"Now, when you say that Andreas, Sam, and Tim started to leave, what do you mean?"

"They were over at the playground that's marked in blue."

"And then what did you see?"

"I saw a bunch of kids comin' down the street, and it looked like the majority had bats or somethin' in their hands. There were at least twenty of them."

"And what did you do after observing the kids coming down Huron Avenue?"

"I got into Scott's car and moved it around the corner onto Grove Street."

"What happened to all the sticks that had been placed near the playground?"

"While Andreas was over at the playground, he must've picked up a stick 'cause he put it in the back seat of Scott's car."

Please, Todd, take Andreas with you, drive away, get out of there, keep moving. PLEASE!

"And then what happened?"

"I moved Scott's car onto Grove Street, then I grabbed a stick out of the back seat and started headin' over to where Tim, Sam, and Andreas were, but a police officer cut me off and told me to put my hands on the hood of his car."

Todd's words instantly brought back images of the day he had briefly stopped by our house not long after Andreas was killed. Both of us had been teary-eyed, still in disbelief at what had happened that Saturday night. We sat in my backyard, in the shade of a tree that bordered the adjacent playground. I could hardly believe what I was hearing. "The officer grabbed the back of my head and hit my face on the hood of the cruiser and asked me where I was going," Todd remembered. "I told him, 'Nowhere,' but he yelled, 'Yeah? You're goin' to jail!'"

I opened my eyes wide and shook my head from side to side. I watched Todd's sad, pained face and continued to listen in horror. "Then he asked me, 'Where are you from?' When I told him I was from Belmont, the officer said, really loud, 'It figures. Stay out of the big city!' He was pullin' my hair, but he let me go after we heard screams."

Turning my attention back to the courtroom, I listened as Mr. Rapacki continued his questioning. "When you encountered the police officer, did you have a stick in your hand?"

"Yes," replied Todd, "the stick Andreas had put in the back seat of the car."

"What kind of stick was it?"

"A broken hockey stick."

"The last time you saw Andreas before that, did he have anything in his hand?"

"No. Like I said, he'd put the stick he had in the car."

"And how long did you spend with the police officer?"

"He asked me a few questions, so prob'ly about three, maybe five, minutes."

"From where you were with the police officer, could you see what was happening at the intersection of Grove and Huron?"

"No. I couldn't see anything."

"So what happened next?"

"There was a lot of screamin', a lot of yellin', a lot of noise comin' from the intersection, so the police officer let me go and ran down there."

"And what did you do?"

"I ran down there too."

"And when you got to the scene, what did you observe?"

"I saw Doug runnin' away; he had blood comin' from his face. And I saw Dylan lyin' in the middle of the street, near the yellow line. He was holdin' his shoulder and his face."

"Now, Doug and Dylan, who are they?"

"Friends of ours who'd also come from the party we went to."

"What else did you see?"

"I saw Andreas over by the driveway of the house next to the golf course. He was on his knees with one hand on the ground and the other hand over his wound."

Todd's words sounded hollow to me, as if they were coming from a distant place. As his words painted a frightening scene, I felt the room begin to spin out of control.

"Did you hear Andreas say anything?"

"He was screamin', but I couldn't really tell what he was sayin'. He was covered with blood."

"And then what did you see?"

"After I realized what had happened, I turned around and saw the police officer standin' there, so I told him to call an ambulance, which he did."

"How long until the ambulance arrived?"

"About five minutes."

"Your Honor, I have no further questions for Mr. Giles," Mr. Rapacki announced.

"OK. Good. Any cross-examination?" the judge asked the defense attorneys.

"Yes, Judge," Mr. Harris replied.

"Go ahead."

—ɱ—

Mr. Harris rose from his chair, and with a flick of his fingers, he pulled open the button of his tight-fitting, dark jacket before reaching the podium. Everybody in the courtroom held their breath.

Will he make Andreas and his friends look like criminals?

"Good afternoon, Mr. Giles. My name is Ronald Harris, and I represent Mr. McCale in reference to this matter. You were a good friend of Mr. Dresp's?"

"Yes, I was," Todd answered.

"And you recall that particular evening vividly, don't you?"

"Yes."

"So you consumed alcohol at the party?"

"Yes, I consumed alcohol at the party."

"Now, Mr. Giles, you testified that when you left Glacken Field, at the municipal parking lot at the golf course, you were chased from there, correct?"

"Yes."

"And after that, you went to Mr. Dresp's home, correct?"

"Yes."

Andreas, please come inside. Come home.

Suddenly, the judge interrupted. "May I see counsel at sidebar? It's one o'clock. Let's break for the day. Mr. Giles, you are excused, but don't discuss your testimony with anybody except Mr. Rapacki, Ms. Sanchez, Mr. Harris, or Mr. Kohl. We'll resume your testimony at nine o'clock tomorrow morning. OK, let me see counsel at the sidebar."

While the lawyers went up to the sidebar, my eyes turned toward the jurors. *These are the people who will decide the fate of the young man accused of killing Andreas.* The faces of the women and men had become increasingly somber over the past few hours.

Before ending the proceedings for the day, the judge said, "Members of the jury, it's very important that you decide the case entirely on what you see and hear during the presentation of the case in the courtroom and out on the view, meaning when we go to the crime scene."

The crime scene? All these people will be going to the place where Andreas suffered so terribly? Can I come along so I can kneel on the pavement where my son's blood was spilled? I want to go but not alone. Will somebody please go with me?

"It's crucial that you not talk to anybody about this case. You shouldn't talk to each other or to anybody else. You also shouldn't read about the case or listen to or watch anything about it. Please be here by quarter to nine tomorrow morning so we can begin at nine o'clock sharp. Thank you very much. See you tomorrow."

"All rise!"

If only they . . . if only . . ., the words kept running through my mind. *How could you all have made such terrible decisions that night?* The jurors, their bodies bent forward a bit as if deep in prayer, left the room, followed by the judge, tall and erect, and the four attorneys. The men and women who had sat to our right on the defendant's side of the benches began to leave through the large wooden door, but Lucy asked us to wait, "Let's let the defendant and his family leave the courtroom first."

Our group left the room last. We followed Lucy into the hallway where she motioned for us to stand to one side. We just stared at each other, speechless. *Is Andreas downstairs or outside with Todd? Is he coming home with us?*

When Mr. Rapacki came out of the courtroom, Robert stopped him and inquired, "How do you think it went today?" I couldn't hear Mr. Rapacki's response. There was no room in my heart or my head for additional information. I just wanted to go home and see whether Andreas had come back. I'd had enough of the courtroom and the trial, but Robert needed to know what Mr. Rapacki thought and what he had planned for the next day. Knowing what to expect was important to Robert. Even if I *had* been able to find some words, asking questions frightened me because I wasn't sure I would get the answers I wanted to hear. I wanted reassurance that the murderer would get locked up for life.

As Lucy walked us to the main door of the courthouse, she asked, "Do you have any more questions that I can answer before you leave?"

"No, we're fine," we both replied at the same time.

"Court resumes tomorrow morning at nine, so let's meet in my office at eight forty-five," she said in her usual calm voice as we started to leave.

"Goodbye. We'll see you tomorrow," said Robert. "Thank you for all your help today."

Leaving the building through the same door we'd entered that morning, Robert and I walked out onto the busy city street. As my eyes adjusted to daylight, my hand, fingers splayed wide, flew involuntarily to my chest. *Wow! The sky is still above me and the ground on which I'm standing still exists!* I looked around and was surprised to see vehicles and pedestrians passing hurriedly by. It seemed unreal that people could be going about their lives as if the horror of Andreas's fate hadn't touched them. *Doesn't everyone know that Andreas is gone? Am I in a waking nightmare? No, this is real—I just survived a day in the presence of the person accused of taking Andreas from us.*

Robert stood next to me in silence, as if also readjusting to the outside world. At first, we didn't speak, but then Robert asked me, "Are you hungry? Do you want to go out to eat?"

"Yes, I'm hungry, but let's not stay around here. I want to get as far away from this place as possible."

After a long ride through heavy traffic down Commonwealth Avenue from Cambridge to Boston, we walked into a familiar Thai restaurant. As if it were our first time there, my eyes jumped all around the room. I noticed the pink tablecloths and small vases of pink and white carnations. My gaze turned to the walls with murals of dancing Thai women, then skipped to the variegated snake plants lined up along the windowsill. Men and women sat at tables with plates of colorful red, green, and white vegetables piled high in front of them. A young businesswoman moved a forkful of rice and broccoli toward her parting lips as her companion leaned in and quietly said something that made her put the fork down and smile. While nothing had changed at the restaurant since I'd last been there, everything had changed in my world. It all felt surreal and very, very strange. *Did we really just come from a murder trial?*

"Would you like to be seated?" a young waiter asked, breaking my trance.

"Yes," I heard Robert say. We followed the waiter in silence to a small table. Wordlessly, Robert and I sat down on the soft seats. After a while, we discussed the menu. Neither of us could decide what to eat, so the waiter helped us choose.

Back home, later that afternoon, I had a strong urge to visit Andreas at the cemetery to tell him about our experiences in court. I wrote him another letter, as I did almost every day.

Thursday, September 28, 1989
Andreas,
I'm here with you after spending the day in court. Your dad is at home. Darkness is moving in over the mature trees and tombstones, but when I turn my head, I'm drawn toward the brilliant orange sunset peeking through the pines. Gazing at such beauty, I imagine you're in that light and here with me now.

Andreas, I survived the first day. I held on to your gold eagle pendant the whole time. It made me feel that you were with me in some way. I have no words to even attempt to ask for your forgiveness; I wasn't able to save you. My body and soul exist in anguish for the way you died.

I think Mr. Rapacki did everything he could to make an impactful opening statement in court today. The judge would not allow a picture of you in the courtroom for fear that it would prejudice the jury. That didn't make sense to me since the accused sat in plain view of the jury. Would that not prejudice the jury seeing him there in person given that he's so young? But Mr. Rapacki repeated your name often and always with a very compassionate tone in his voice. He humanized you and gave you a presence in the courtroom.

Andreas, it has become quite dark and a bit frightening to me here alone among the tombstones; I can barely see the lines in my notebook. When I get home, I'm going to call Tom at

UMass to see if he wants to come to the trial tomorrow. So far, he has not wanted to attend. He feels rage toward your murderer and does not want to see him in person.

I will wear your gold eagle necklace to court again tomorrow to keep you present throughout the day and to give me strength and protection.

Loving you and missing you forever,

Mom

CHAPTER 8

Day Two

Friday, September 29, the second day of the trial, was cool and overcast. Robert and I knew that we'd hear more about the last moments of Andreas's life. Robert put on his navy-blue blazer and gray pants and a different tie than the day before, just as he would vary them when going to work. His face looked hard, as if his muscles had turned into knots under his white, suddenly aged skin.

Before leaving the house, I again fastened Andreas's eagle pendant around my neck. Alongside it hung the gold locket my friends had given me for my forty-fourth birthday—the first one without Andreas—just days after his death.

Are we going to sit by Andreas as he suffers and then he'll come home with us? I knew I would soon see him come for a short weekend visit from his sophomore year of college since he was only about forty-five minutes away from home. He would throw his green duffel bag, lightly packed with books and clothes, into the corner of our dining room before making his way to the kitchen to see what was simmering on the stovetop or to search our freezer for his favorite vanilla-flavored Brigham's ice cream.

As we neared the courthouse, my breathing became shallow and my heart banged loudly inside the silent car. *Where are we going to park our car today? There's no space on the street.* Just then, a car pulled out of a parking space to our right. *Andreas, did you do that for us?*

After we met Lucy in her office, we made our way to the sixth floor. Outside Courtroom B, Lucy said in her naturally soothing voice, "Wait right here while I check to make sure the defendant and his team have settled in." Soon, she returned to us in the dimly lit corridor. "The defendant's family is sitting on the bench, just inside the door," she said. "We'll take the same seats we had yesterday." Lucy motioned away from where the defendant's family sat and pointed toward the opposite end of the bench. "We'll sit there." Robert and I followed Lucy back into the nightmare—this trial, this play, this Shakespearean tragedy. Had we ever left?

I hesitated before stepping back into the courtroom. As if Andreas were still in the hospital's recovery room, I had the momentary feeling that I should tiptoe to my seat so as not to awaken my sleeping son. As Lucy led the way, we followed a narrow aisle between the defendant's table and the spectators' gallery. From the corner of my eye, I caught a glimpse of the accused seated next to his attorney at the defendant's table. In that instant, I felt like a cloud of very dense air lifted my body off the ground, causing it to hover above. I observed from outside myself how my newly aged, colorless face was in sharp contrast to the black blouse I wore. I also saw the mother of the accused sitting in silence in the second row. I wanted his mother and his other family members to show remorse, but they just sat watching their attorneys trying to get the defendant to walk out the door a free man. Once I reached the other end of the wooden bench, I took my seat between Robert and Lucy.

Andreas, can you be with us and Todd as he testifies today? I silently pleaded. As I reached my right hand toward my neck where Andreas's eagle pendant hung, I felt a rush of warm air encircle my body.

"All rise!" the bailiff commanded. Simultaneously, everyone in the courtroom stood in absolute silence. The immense room felt empty for a moment.

"Good morning, ladies and gentlemen," the judge greeted after we all sat down. "Would every member of the jury who has obeyed the court's instructions not to talk about this case, not to read about this case, and not to listen to or watch anything about this case please raise her or his hand?

"OK. It appears that every member of the jury has obeyed the court's instructions. Thank you. We can resume. Mr. Giles, I will remind you that you are still under oath. Mr. Harris, you may resume cross-examination."

"Thank you, Your Honor," the defense attorney acknowledged.

With his left eye twitching, Todd once again took the witness stand. The defense attorney, his dark jacket already unbuttoned, took a few quick steps toward the podium and immediately fired his first question.

"I believe yesterday just before we left off, you had testified that you and your friends had gone to Mr. Dresp's home. Now, Mr. Giles, while you and your friends were at Mr. Dresp's home, did any of you go inside and call the police to tell them you'd been threatened?"

"No."

"And that's because you all felt safe since you were no longer being chased, correct?"

"That's correct."

Please Andreas and Todd, come inside. I'm in the kitchen. Andreas, please come home. I'm waiting for you. Please, tell me what's going on. What made you so angry? Was it something those strangers said to you? Can't you just walk away? They have nothing to do with you. Don't go back to the field, please.

"But you and your friends decided to go into the garage?"

"Yes."

"And while you were in the garage, Mr. Giles, did you or some of your friends decide to arm yourselves with certain weapons?"

"Yes."

"And remind me, what were those weapons?"

"Cutoff hockey sticks and broomsticks."

Weapons? The defense attorney's questions forced me to see our son and his best friend opening our garage door and taking out cut-off sticks I didn't even know they had.

"And you knew that these cutoff sticks could be used to injure someone, correct?"

"Yes."

"You selected them for the purpose of inflicting injury on another person, correct?"

"Correct."

Andreas and Todd as the attackers? How can the defense attorney bring up details that make my son and Todd look like attackers? How can he make Andreas's friend so uncomfortable? Has Todd not suffered enough having lost his best friend on the street?

"Who else picked up weapons?"

"Andreas, Mike, and Tim."

"You were armed with weapons then, correct?"

"Yes."

"And you walked to the playground, right?"

"Yes."

"The four of you were intent on going back there, right?"

"Yes."

"And you hid those weapons in a location that you could easily get them later on, right?"

"Yes."

Did the devil possess you guys? How did the thought of fighting with strangers even enter your minds? Why didn't one of you say, "Let's just get out of here and go home"? Please, can one of you say it? Please. My silent begging had no impact on the development of the scene being described. It did not stop the flow of sequential images and the string of decisions our son and his friends made, moving them closer and closer to danger just down the street from our house.

"Now, you and your friends crossed Grove Street. Is that correct, Mr. Giles?"

"Yes."

"And when you entered the golf course, is it fair to say that there's a pathway?"

"Yes."

"And the pathway, it's hidden from view, isn't it?"

"Yes."

"Then you and your friends made another decision, didn't you, Mr. Giles?"

"Yes."

"You and your friends all decided that you wanted more people with you, correct?"

"Correct."

"And Mr. Dresp agreed with that?"

"Yes. But he waited there."

I wanted to shake my head, but I had to forcefully keep it still so as not to prejudice the jury. Those images contradicted my view of my son and his friends. I kept staring at Todd's lips to see what else he had to say.

Andreas is still alive. He is willing to fight alongside his friends. Please, Andreas, turn around. Come home!

"Whose idea was it to get more people?"

"Nobody's specifically."

"Who stayed behind?"

"Andreas and Tim."

"When you guys left them behind, you went to a party in Belmont, correct?"

"Yes."

"But when you went to the party, you didn't go there to dance or listen to music or meet any girls, correct?"

"Correct."

"You went there to recruit other young men for a fight?"

"Yes."

"Because you were real mad, weren't you?" Mr. Harris said with a note of sarcasm in his voice.

"Yes."

"And Mr. Dresp was real mad, too, wasn't he?"

"Yes."

"Now, Mr. Giles, while you guys were at the party enlisting more young men to fight, it's fair to say that you don't know what Mr. Dresp was doing, correct?"

"That's correct."

"So you don't know if he went back to the playground and picked up any of the weapons you guys had hidden, do you?"

"No."

"How many young men did you bring back from the party to fight?"

"We brought back nine."

He's talking about Andreas and his friends, isn't he? It just doesn't fit. They've never been in a fight. What happened?

"When you got back from the party with more people, where did you go?"

"To the golf course."

"Where was Mr. Dresp?"

"He was still on the pathway by the house next to the golf course."

"Hidden from view?"

"Yes."

"Now, sir, when you got back to the parking lot was anybody there?"

"Yes."

"When you returned to the parking lot, how many people were there?"

"Maybe six or seven. As far as I could tell, they were from—"

"Did you fight with them?" the defense attorney interrupted before Todd could finish his sentence.

"No, we didn't."

"Did you turn around?"

"Yes, when the police showed up."

"And did you or one of your friends tell the police that somebody had threatened you guys with a baseball bat?"

"No."

"What *did* you do?"

"We ran away, back up to the pathway by the house on the golf course."

"And it's fair to say that you stayed there until the police left, correct?"

"Yes."

"At some point, did you return to the entranceway to the golf course?"

"Yes."

"Were you still expecting to fight with the boys you believed to be from Cambridge?"

"We were at first, but after a few minutes, we thought they'd left, so we started walkin' up Huron Avenue to leave."

"And Mr. Dresp still had his hockey stick in his hands?"

"At that time, I . . . I'm actually not sure."

"You don't know?"

"No, I don't."

"You don't know whether he was still carrying his weapon, right?"

"Correct."

Weapon! Andreas, Todd, weapons? Those words don't fit together!

"Now, Mr. Giles, when you arrived at Huron Avenue, what did you do?"

"Brian said they were comin' back, so he ran out into the street where there was a white car with some kids in it. When we got to the street, the kids got back into the white car when they saw us. Then they left. But there was another car in the cemetery."

"There was another car in the cemetery?"

"Yes, with a bunch of kids."

"Mr. Giles, you didn't see Mr. Dresp put that hockey stick in the back seat of that car, did you?"

"Yes, I did!" Todd said emphatically.

"But you and your friends left, didn't you? At that time?"

"Yeah. We waited there in the street for about five minutes, and then a bunch of kids came down. After Andreas put the stick in the back seat of Scott's car, I moved it up the road."

"You didn't see any fighting?"

"No."

"And you don't know what Mr. Dresp was doing when he was wounded, do you?"

"No, I don't."

"When you said that you were stopped by a police officer, was it a Cambridge officer or a Belmont officer?"

"Cambridge."

"And where was that officer coming from?"

"He turned right off of Huron and went north on Grove Street."

"Thank you, Mr. Giles. Your Honor, I have no further questions for this witness."

Andreas, please come home. Please.

After Mr. Rapacki asked Todd a few redirect questions, the judge excused Todd from the witness stand. He slowly stepped down from the platform with his head held high, then his parents followed him out of the courtroom.

"Next witness, please."

A teenager with the stature of a football player stepped into the witness stand and was introduced to the court as a friend of the defendant. *What a big, scary-looking kid!* I thought as Mr. Rapacki began his line of questioning. *He's only seventeen?* I knew this was the person who had menacingly twirled a baseball bat as he asked Andreas and his friends if they had passes to enter Glacken Field that night. As he answered each question, the sound of the witness's voice transported me to the parking lot at the golf course next to Glacken Field. I could see the young men as they gathered under the lights that illuminated the parking lot. *Run away and come home, Andreas! It's late at night. Don't you see the danger you're in? He's twirling a baseball bat! He's threatened you and your friends. Run! Come home!! Please, Andreas, please leave!*

Despite my pleading, what was done could never be undone. The witness provided more and more details about what he saw during the fight. Eventually, I could only hear the sound of his voice. It was like I wasn't in the courtroom at all but was watching the events unfold from someplace faraway. The scenes this witness described were more than my overwhelmed psyche and inconsolable heart could absorb that day, and so later, I only remembered his testimony as fragmented and slow-moving, unsettling but strangely devoid of detail. Perhaps my soul protected me from hearing more than I could bear on that day.

When the judge ordered a brief recess, my gaze followed him and the jurors as they filed out, disappearing one by one through a doorway at the front of the courtroom. My body numb, I could neither silence the witness's description of Andreas's screams nor erase the brutal images of his death from my mind.

Lucy accompanied Robert and me to a quiet corner. *Where am I? What's happening? Can it be that Andreas was really taken from us in such a horrific way?* I glanced across the corridor where a large group of people had gathered and noticed the petite woman from the day before. I remembered her telling me that she wanted her son to meet me. I watched as she stepped away from the group and made her way toward me, trailed by a young man a full head taller than her.

"Hi, I want my son to meet you," she said assertively. Then she quickly turned her head toward her son and said, "This is the victim's mother. I want you to greet her."

The young man slowly extended his right hand toward me. Startled, I suddenly felt his strong but clammy hand in mine. "Nice to meet you," he said shyly, quickly averting his eyes. *Whose hand am I touching?* I wondered. *Did this hand harm Andreas?* I felt my heart drop.

"I hope this will turn his life around!" his mother exclaimed before she and her son retreated down the corridor. I could not command my eyes to look away as I watched mother and son blend into the group across the hallway. I kept staring for what seemed like a long time. *Mother and son still together. Mother and son.*

"We need to get back. The trial will resume soon," Lucy said with a sense of urgency.

A few minutes later, Mr. Rapacki called his next witness. *Oh my God, it's him! His mother just introduced us. I just shook his hand! I can't believe it. Is he the one who fought with Andreas? Will he tell the truth of what he saw and did?* As the witness approached the stand, I noticed he was now wearing a striped suit jacket over the black T-shirt he'd been wearing when he clasped my hand in the hallway. As he lifted his right arm to be sworn in, the stripes on the azure-blue jacket sleeve shimmered in the artificial light of the courtroom.

"Sir, in a loud, clear voice so all the jurors can hear you, please state your name and age," Mr. Rapacki requested.

"My name is Kevin Smith, and I'm twenty-one years old."

In spite of the prosecutor's request, the witness spoke in a near whisper. *Does he not want us to hear what he has to say? Does he not want to hear it himself?* Though a part of me didn't want to take in the barely audible words that came from this young man's reluctant lips as he began to testify, I was unable to look away. I closely watched his face in expectation since he had sworn, "to tell the truth, the whole truth, and nothing but the truth." Gradually, as Mr. Rapacki reminded him to speak up, I was able to hear more of this witness's testimony—yet the more I was able to hear, the greater my need to escape the brutality of what was being described.

After the witness stepped down from the stand, the judge issued another recess and the bailiff called out, "All rise!" My body stood up automatically, then Robert and I followed Lucy out the door for a short break. After she made sure the defendant and his camp were on the other side of the corridor, she said, "I'll be right back." Robert and I stood in a quiet corner, each of us alone with our thoughts. Needing to use the restroom, I walked toward it as if floating. Pulling open the old door, I was surprised to see a line of chatting women waiting for a stall. The chatter stopped the instant I entered the room.

When it was my turn, I went into a stall and latched the metal door behind me. I could hear women murmuring through the door, but I couldn't make out what they were saying. Suddenly, I wondered, *Who is on the other side of this stall? Is it the defendant's mother or one of his other relatives? How strange to be so close to them, to the ones on the other end of the courtroom bench.*

On my way back to the corridor, it hit me that we were all a part of the same play, we were just hoping for different endings. When I returned, Robert was standing with some of the parents of Andreas's friends. Lucy arrived just in time to walk us back into the courtroom.

After the judge told us to be seated, he said to Mr. Rapacki, "You may resume direct examination."

The prosecutor's straightforward questions and the witness's hesitant responses moved me back through space and time to the night in question. I found myself watching a group of young men at the basketball court near the Charles River in Cambridge. I could see the pack of beer placed at the side of the court and the players pivoting as they maneuvered to get the ball through the hoop.

At the same time, I kept replaying images of Andreas getting dressed to go out with his friends on that last night of his life. *Please, Andreas, don't go to the park. Come home! Bring your friends along, please!*

"Just before the break, Mr. Smith, you were telling us how you came to leave the basketball court in Cambridge with your friends, including the defendant," Mr. Rapacki continued. "Please pick up where you left off."

"Yeah, as I was sayin', the sun was beginnin' to set, makin' it too dark for us to continue playin'," I heard Kevin Smith say.

Wait until the floodlights come on. Please continue to play. Don't leave the basketball court.

"So we left the court and went to Harvard Square where we ran into some guys we knew from school. But hangin' out at the Square wasn't much fun, so we decided to go visit a friend who lives further uptown."

Please, stay in the Square. Don't come up by where we live. Turn around and go the other way, please—please!

As if watching a movie or TV show, I kept seeing images of Andreas and his friends playing games at the carnival where Andreas's friend Mike met the girl. *Please don't invite him to meet you at Glacken Field later*, I begged this unknown girl. *Please tell him and his friends to stay where they are.*

As questioning continued, the courtroom was thick with tension. All eyes were on Kevin Smith. He wasn't just the defendant's close friend, he was also the only person with the defendant and Andreas when Andreas was attacked. "What happened after you started walking down Huron Avenue?" Mr. Rapacki asked the witness.

Please stop the reel. Andreas, please come home now. Don't stay on the street.

"A police cruiser passed us, and someone yelled, 'Cruiser,' so I threw my weapons to the side of the road."

"What kind of weapons did you have?"

"A broomstick, a beer bottle, and a knife."

"And where along the side of the road did you throw them?"

"To the left side of the road as I faced Grove Street."

Andreas, please run away. Please, run! Come home. I'm sitting in the kitchen waiting for you. Bring your friends along.

The next thing I knew, the witness was describing how he was wrestling and fighting with Andreas. "We got ahold of each other and neither of us would let go," he said. "We wrestled down the street away from where everybody else was fightin' until we were almost at the intersection of Huron and Grove. I saw Corey and yelled at him to help me. Corey came toward me after I called out to him. He had his hand behind his belt, like he was reachin' for somethin'."

Get away from Andreas! Keep that hand inside your pants, behind your belt. Don't move it.

"What happened next?" Mr. Rapacki asked.

"Corey came up from behind him and suddenly Andreas Dresp screamed."

"Mr. Smith, please state the full name of the person who helped you and point him out to the jury."

"It's Corey McCale. He's sittin' right there at the table between the two lawyers. He's wearin' a pin-striped suit and tie and a white shirt," the witness answered in his barely audible voice.

"Please note that the witness has pointed to the defendant, Mr. McCale," the prosecutor said. "What happened after you heard Andreas Dresp scream?"

"I said to Corey, 'Get his hands off me!' 'cause Andreas had ahold of my shirt and I couldn't get loose."

"After you said that to the defendant, what happened?"

"Corey punched him in the face."

"How many times did the defendant punch Andreas in the face?"

"I don't know the exact number, but it was a few."

I felt my facial bones crack under my skin, feeling each blow to Andreas's face. Knowing that any sign of emotion was forbidden in the courtroom, I used every ounce of my strength to hold back the torrent of tears that wanted to flow.

"And then what happened?"

"I was still wrestlin' with Andreas, so Corey picked a stick up off the ground and hit him in the head. Then Andreas let go."

Suddenly, in the midst of Kevin Smith's testimony, a part of me began to drift upward toward the courtroom's high ceiling and away from my body, which sat grounded and motionless on the hard bench.

Feeling oddly detached, I felt myself floating above my frozen body as the prosecutor finished his questioning and sat down. As the defense attorney moved to the podium and began his cross-examination, I hovered above him, numbly watching the scene unfold.

"Now, Mr. Smith, you testified on direct examination that you were going down Huron Avenue when you heard someone say the word *cruiser*. Is that correct?" Mr. Harris asked.

"That's correct."

"And at that point, you disposed of the knife you'd been carrying, right?"

"Correct."

"And you also disposed of the beer bottle and the broomstick you were going to use as weapons?"

"That's right."

"But you still walked down the hill?"

"Yes."

"Even though the police were right there?"

"No, they had already left."

"When they left and drove by you, how many people were with you walking down the street?"

Andreas is still alive! Officer, please stop. Please turn on your flashing lights. Please. Please!

"About fifteen."

"And there were another fifteen people at the end of the street, right?"

"That's right."

"And did they have weapons?"

"Yes, they did."

"So the fifteen people you were with were marching toward the fifteen people at the other end of the street, and although you had dropped your weapons, some of the people with you were armed, correct?"

"That's right."

"And the police cruiser just drove right on by your group?"

"Correct."

"And it never stopped?"

"No, sir, it did not."

"Did the police officers ever exit their vehicle and take away the sticks that the other people were carrying?"

"No, they didn't."

"But you, Mr. Smith, had disposed of your weapons before the fight?" the defense attorney asked with cynical suspicion.

"That's right."

I shook my head invisibly to wake myself up from this nightmare, but to no avail.

"I have no further questions, Your Honor."

As the witness walked past me, a cool breeze whipped by my legs. I stared at Kevin Smith's back until he disappeared behind the large wooden door. Then the entire courtroom began to spin, and my body seemed to disconnect from the ground. Like old slides in a carousel, images of the attack on Andreas clicked through my mind, one after another. *Andreas, how much you had to suffer, so much, so much. How much you had to endure!*

Although my body was frozen to the bench, my eyes were highly alert, capturing everything that was taking place in the courtroom. *Is this what happens in moments of terror, our psyche processes everything in slow motion, in the utmost detail?* I saw some movement at the defendant's table, where Corey McCale sat with his lawyers. As he turned his head toward his attorney, I noticed his neat hairline near the nape of his neck, like he'd just gotten a haircut for this occasion. *What I wouldn't give to trim Andreas's hair, to softly lay my hand upon his neck just one more time, even just for a second!*

My gaze followed the accused as he tilted his head and whispered something into his attorney's ear. The back of the attorney's jacket crumpled as he protectively placed his arm around the shoulder of his young client. *Is he comforting him? Did the attorney hear what the*

witness said his client did to my son? Can I hear Andreas whisper into
my ear one last time? Please, just one more time? Could I please put my
arm around Andreas's shoulder, even if just to say goodbye?

The detective who oversaw the homicide unit and took the lead
in Andreas's case was scheduled to testify next. Knowing the detective would go into detail about the crime and feeling we'd reached
our limit, Robert and I decided we'd heard enough for the day. As we
walked out of the courthouse and to our car, Andreas's pain, the brutality of the attack upon him, and the knowledge that he would never
return home hung like lead chains around my heart.

—ᴍ—

After listening to the day's testimony, I stopped at the cemetery to be
with Andreas. As I sat beside his burial spot, I opened the journal I'd
brought with me, pulled a pen from my pocket, and began to write.

Friday, September 29, 1989
My dear Andreas,
I just came to take care of your flowers and to be close to you.
The sky is bright blue today with not a cloud in sight. You
would love to see the trees swaying in the softly blowing wind
and hear the birdsong over the rustle of the leaves. I miss you
with all my heart. I can barely endure the agony of how painfully and senselessly you had to leave this world.

Andreas, I can't stay very long because I must get ready for
our trip to New Hampshire. In a few hours, your dad, Julia, and
I are going to the White Mountains. We are hoping that the
beauty of the wilderness will give us the strength to go on. We
are also hoping that it will help us erase the images and sounds
of what we have heard happened to you—or at least dilute them
so we can continue to attend the trial.

Andreas, you were in everybody's heart today as we listened to the way you were butchered to death. The pain of your suffering has torn my heart into shreds. I can't imagine that it will ever mend or stop bleeding.

With all my love forever,

Mom

CHAPTER 9

Mountains

Having made it through the first two days of the trial, Robert, Julia, and I headed north late on Friday afternoon. We moved along the same highway Robert and I had driven so many times with our sons before Andreas's death. Now everything was different. Speeding past the red and golden maple trees, I could sense the movement of time. Was it the sensation of Andreas staying behind in the summer while my life continued into autumn that made the passing of time so tangible, so utterly real? Yet, at the same time, a part of me couldn't escape the feeling that life was going about its normal course—that Tom and Andreas had returned to their colleges for the fall semester and Robert and I would soon welcome them home for a long weekend.

The sun was setting when we arrived at our hotel near the base of Mount Washington in New Hampshire. A line of gray clouds tinged with an orange glow lit up the horizon, and a cool mountain breeze greeted us as we opened our car doors. As I stepped out of the car and placed my feet onto the crunchy gravel parking lot, I was instantly transported to another day when Tom and Andreas were still in elementary school. Robert and I had taken the boys, as we often did during summer vacations, to Schroon Lake in the beautiful Adirondacks, in eastern New York, where Robert's parents had a cottage on the water. *The boys must already be down at the lake. That's the first thing they do when we arrive at the cottage.*

"Let's check in," Robert said, interrupting the memory. The three of us carried our bags from the car into the hotel, which was surrounded by sugar maple, red oak, birch, and white pine trees. We unpacked our cooler with the potato salad I had made for supper, along with bread, butter, jelly, and boiled eggs for breakfast. We made plans to leave the next morning at sunrise to get an early start on our hike. *This feels so normal. What a relief to be away from the city. But why the loud banging of my heart and the throbbing throughout my body?*

The next day when I smelled the fresh mountain air, my heart rejoiced. My senses took everything in. The morning fog gave the mountain a dreamy appearance. Robert, Julia, and I began our walk in silence toward an arbor of small green leaves. I felt drawn into it as if a heavenly force were calling me to feel the softness of the pine needles on the ground and see the fiery autumn leaves in shades of ruby, amber, and cinnamon at the end of the path.

Are we receiving a gift from another dimension of life? Is it a gift from God? Since Andreas's death, the colors and shapes of flowers and trees, the singing of birds, and the rustling of leaves had all become miraculous hidden forces that helped strengthen my broken heart. *Andreas, have you become part of these earthly yet heavenly inspired sights and sounds?*

Soon, the narrow path opened to reveal a splendid view. Puffy white clouds floated through the vast robin's-egg-blue sky. In the distance, flaming orange and red bushes circled a glistening pond, a fiery blaze against the dark pine forest. In awe, we stopped to take it all in. *Andreas, did you lead us here to remind us of the splendor in this world?*

In silence, we continued our walk at a slower pace up the rocky mountain trail. After a few hours of hiking, we stopped again. The beauty of the majestic mountains and the patches of vibrant colors below were mesmerizing. Each of us peered into the distance, lost in our own thoughts and sensations. I inhaled a deep breath and thought, *We have to come here with Tom and Andreas. I want them to see this beauty.*

Beyond the tree line the vegetation changed, with the towering hardwood trees giving way to smaller conifers, dwarf shrubs, and alpine flowers. I looked up toward the vast blue sky and wondered, *Are we getting closer to heaven? Is this where you are, Andreas?* As the path narrowed and became steeper, we were forced to walk single file. I felt an invisible thread pulling me upward and keeping me safe.

"I can't wait to reach the top," I said to Julia, who was hiking between me and Robert. I'd noticed her expression becoming more and more serene with each step she took. She loved to be in the mountains.

Robert was walking a short distance ahead of us. Suddenly, I heard footsteps coming up behind me, so I turned my head to see who it was. *Is it Andreas catching up to us?* My heart leaped with anticipation, but then I remembered, *Oh no, it's not him! I'll never see him again.* As my knees began to shake and my heart started pounding, I immediately sat down on a grassy spot and leaned against a boulder. Robert and Julia stopped further up the path and looked back at me after a few hikers passed us by.

"Are you OK?" Robert called to me.

"Yes, but I can't continue going up. My knees are too wobbly. You two go ahead. I'll go back down to the tree line."

"OK, we won't be long," Robert called reassuringly from a distance.

As I backtracked down the trail, I searched for a secluded spot where I could listen to the sounds of the wildlife without the voices of hikers disturbing me. Stepping away from the main path, I saw a bright green patch of moss at the base of a tall tree. I bent down to feel its softness, then sat down next to it on the trunk of a felled tree. As the wind whispered through the leaves, my anxious heart began to calm. Suddenly, a loud rustling disturbed the harmony. Fear glued my body to the tree trunk as I watched a man with a large knife coming toward me as if in slow motion. I jumped up and rushed past the startled middle-aged man toward the main path, where a group of young hikers was coming up the trail.

No sooner were they out of sight than tears of rage poured down my face. Before Andreas was killed, I would've recognized that rustling in the woods as chipmunks chasing each other through the dry leaves and the man as simply another hiker. He didn't even have a knife; it was fear that triggered the image, a traumatic remnant from what I'd heard at the trial.

Before long, Robert and Julia returned for me. As we headed back down the mountain, my body was still shaking. *How could I let myself be defeated so quickly? I allowed the murderer to intrude, even in this heavenly place.* Walking through a woodsy area where a canopy of statuesque trees blocked the tall mountain peaks and billowing clouds, I said, "I don't want to go back yet. I'd like to continue hiking and see more views."

Julia knew her way through the woods. Pointing toward a winding path to our left, she suggested, "Let's try this other trail; maybe it's not as steep." We wordlessly changed course and continued along, hearing only the crunch of our boots on gravel and the occasional chatter of hikers with backpacks passing by. *Tom and Andreas are at home. They are spending time with their friends.*

Gradually, as we moved up higher, the trail narrowed, and we again had to walk single file. After a while, we stopped to rest and take in the view of the mountain range around us and the expansive valley below. Looking down, I admired the mountain's shadow on one side of the valley and the warm glow of the sun illuminating a patch of pine trees on the other.

As I followed Robert and Julia, we approached an area with its steep, rocky slope exposed. Immediately, I slowed down and moved closer toward the rocky mountainside, eager to have something to hold onto. As I gained purchase along the narrow trail, I fixed my gaze on the path before me. Robert and Julia slowed ahead of me as they came upon a young man trying to inch his way down the trail. As he nervously held on to outcroppings of bushes and the rocky ledge of the mountainside, Robert and Julia stepped around him. I tried to do the same, but instead, I froze beside him. Robert reached out his hand to help me pass the young man, but an overwhelming sense of fear had taken over my body. Unable to move, I encouraged Robert and Julia to go ahead.

As we gazed toward the mountain with our backs to the wide-open view before us, the young man and I soon started talking. "Don't look down, just look straight ahead," he told me.

"Your feet are on solid ground," I reminded him, which helped me concentrate as well. "Just take one small step at a time." Eventually, the young man and I were able to inch our way back to the wider path where we continued to talk.

"I'm a pilot and look at me—suddenly afraid of heights," he said with a chuckle.

"Then how do you fly?"

"Well, that's different. In an airplane, I sit in a cabin."

"Oh, yes, I feel the same. I love to look out the window when I'm on board an airplane. It doesn't bother me at all to look down."

"I go to flight school at Daniel Webster College not far from here."

"Oh! That's the college my son's best friend attends. Do you know Todd Giles?"

"Is he tall and real slender with light brown hair?"

"Yes."

"Yeah. He's one of the guys who organized the Oktoberfest at our college this year," he said, smiling. But then suddenly, his face changed, and he remained silent for a moment.

"That Oktoberfest is a fundraiser in my son's memory," I said, wondering if I was revealing too much.

"Are you Andreas's mother?"

"Yes."

"Oh, I remember Andreas. I know what happened to him. It was a big thing on campus."

"Hi, we're back," Robert and Julia announced, interrupting our conversation.

"I'll move on," said the young man.

Tell me more about Andreas, I yearned to say. *What do you remember about him?* My eyes followed the young man as he set out down the shady path.

Afternoon sun was creating more shadows along the path. I watched as groups of other hikers headed down the trail toward the mountain's base. Robert and Julia spoke with delight as they told me about the sights I'd missed further up the trail. But by then, all three of us were tired and, having been on the mountain since early that morning, I said, "Let's go down. I assume we're all getting hungry."

We turned around and let our feet carry us back to the base as swiftly moving dark clouds rushed over us. I wanted to stay in the mountains to have nature talk to me. I also wanted to hear more about Andreas from the young man I'd met on the trail.

The next morning, we took a few short hikes around the smaller hills and meadows. I often glanced toward the young men of Andreas's age who were lying on the green fields next to their girlfriends, soaking in the last warm rays of the autumn sun. Soon, we were back on the highway, the mountains growing smaller behind us until we could no longer see them. We drove in silence, Robert and I knowing we were returning to a world where only one son, instead of two, would greet us when we phoned. We also knew that neither of us would be going back to work the next day. Instead, come morning, we'd make the drive to the courthouse and endure hearing every detail of Andreas's violent death.

Neither of us wanted to do that. We both yearned to return to our regular lives. We wanted our family of four. We wanted Andreas back.

That evening, after Robert and I came home from our trip to the mountains, I penned another letter.

Sunday, October 1, 1989
Dear Andreas,
It's Sunday night. I can't stand the pain of your absence any-more. I don't know what to do.

Andreas, today as I saw so many young people hiking and enjoying themselves in the mountains, I became very angry. I was full of rage at you and your friends. Why did you have to drink alcohol at your age? Why did you have to just hang out rather than go hiking, see the beauty of the world, or do other things? Why did you have to pick up sticks from our garage and then go back to the place where you'd been threatened by guys you didn't even know? I could scream and never stop when I think about the decisions you and your friends made that night.

Now I sit in your untouched room, on the bed you will never again rest your head on, writing to you when what I want with every fiber of my being is to touch you, to see you walk by me in your flannel pajamas at bedtime, to simply say good night and know that I will find you safely in your room the next morning. I just want to see you. You will always be with me in spirit, but I want you physically here with us again. I can't bear this pain of missing you. I will love you forever.
Mom

CHAPTER 10

Day Three

O n Monday, October 2, as we walked into the courtroom and
made our way to our seats, I saw the blank face of the mother
of the accused out of the corner of my eye. Although I kept my head
bowed toward the floor, I noticed that, as usual, she was sitting among
a group of women.

While waiting for the judge and the jurors, I couldn't help but
look in the direction of the defense team, even though I'd been trying
hard to ignore them. I noticed the two lawyers, one on either side of
the accused, place an arm behind their young client's shoulders. They
leaned toward him and whispered into his ears.

*I can never again whisper into Andreas's ear! I'll never see his father
put his arms around his shoulders. Never again, never again.*

"All rise!" The bailiff's booming voice chased away my thoughts.
I abruptly shifted my focus toward the jurors, who were taking their
assigned seats.

Lucy had prepared us for the day. First, the jurors, the lawyers,
and the judge would go view the scene of the crime. After that, the
court would hear again from the detective who had begun his testimony on Friday, and then Brian, one of Andreas's closest friends,
would take the stand.

"Now here's what's going to happen," the judge announced after
the initial formalities. "Court officers will be accompanying us on what
is referred to as a 'jury view of the scene.' These officers will first take
an oath that dates back to the eighteenth century, which allows them

to accompany the jury on this outing. After the officers are sworn in, we'll go downstairs and take buses over to the crime scene. While we're there, you won't hear any testimony or see any evidence, but you may gain a better understanding of how the sequence of events unfolded in this crime.

"It doesn't appear that the rain will cause us any inconvenience. We're all hearty New Englanders, so we shouldn't have a problem with that. While we're at the crime scene, stay close together and don't straggle," the judge continued. "If there's somewhere you want to go or something you want to see, let the officers know. After that, we'll come back here and resume hearing testimony."

What will they do at the place where Andreas suffered the most unbearable pain of his life? Will they step on his blood? Will they gape at the spot like tourists? Will anybody pray for Andreas? I want to go so I can kneel on the street the way Andreas knelt screaming when he was no longer able to stand up. I don't want people to walk on or cars to run over his blood.

Since Andreas's death, every time I had attempted to make the short walk to that place by myself, a heavy force pushed me back toward home. *Does Andreas not want me to go there? Would a car coming around the corner not see me kneeling in the street and run me over? Where exactly on the street was Andreas butchered to death?*

At the sound of the bailiff's now familiar voice, we stood up as the expressionless jurors filed out of the room. Supporters of the defendant followed like a slow-moving stream. Finally, Robert and I stood along with Lucy and the parents of Andreas's friends. We exited silently, our shoulders bent in supplication like congregants approaching an altar for Communion.

As we waited in the corridor for the travelers to return, family members and friends of the accused paced up and down on their side of the hallway, while others leaned against the wall. Robert and I stood on our side and stared vacantly into space. *We're all attending the same trial, yet we need to act like we don't have anything to do with each other. Aren't we all waiting for the same people to return so the trial can resume? When it's over, Robert and I will go home and see Andreas resting in his bed.*

A few times, I sensed some of the defendant's supporters gaping at me. But when I returned their gaze, they looked away. *Should I approach the defendant's mother? What would I say to her?* I wanted to know why her son killed Andreas as I assumed he had, but I couldn't bring myself to ask her that. The social worker in me wished to walk over and listen to what she had endured as the mother of an accused murderer. But I shook my head as if to shake off the thoughts. *Don't go talk to her. You are here because Andreas was murdered, and her son is accused of killing him,* I reminded myself.

"They're back from the viewing," Lucy announced. "Court will resume in a few minutes."

What did the jurors see? Maybe they didn't see anything. Perhaps, like one of the operas or theater productions I've been to, the actors will come out and Andreas will appear now. They will all take a deep bow to the audience's great applause. That's how I'll know that Andreas wasn't really murdered that Saturday night in June.

Soon, I was back in the courtroom, sitting between Robert and Lucy, waiting for the trial to continue. *How much more of this can I hear? How much longer can I sit silently, listening to the details of how my dear son walked, second by second, toward his brutal death? I can only bear witness to my child's suffering and death through the words of his friends because I wasn't there with him as he was dying. I couldn't comfort him. I couldn't even say goodbye. Being present now is the least I can do for Andreas.*

Andreas, can you sense that your mom, your dad, and your friends who love you dearly are with you in the safety of the courtroom, even though none of us could stop the attack?

When the trial resumed, the lead detective was first on the witness stand. Listening to the start of his testimony, I was drawn deeper into the darkness of that Saturday night. I could picture Andreas with his friends, alive at the park near our house, yet I knew he would soon face death. As I focused on the detective—who, dressed in business attire, looked more like an accountant than someone who worked homicide cases—my heart collapsed in on itself and my mind shut down. It was as if my whole being had taken flight to protect me from the detective's heartbreakingly detailed testimony.

Lucy could see my distress and led me out of the oppressive courtroom. In the corridor, she stood close by, and the kindness in her eyes helped me push aside the unbearable images that the detective's statements conjured. Lucy's presence was both grounding and reassuring as she reiterated that I need not listen to everything being said in the trial and could choose to step away at any time. After a few minutes, I felt composed enough to return to the courtroom. Following Lucy back to our seats, I was relieved to see that the detective was no longer on the witness stand. In his place sat Brian Walsh, Andreas's longtime friend, who was with him the night he was killed. He was already responding to Mr. Rapacki's questions.

"After you left Andreas's house, where did you go?" Mr. Rapacki asked Brian.

"We walked over to the golf course and went up the hill to hang out in the parking lot near the clubhouse."

"And when you climbed up the hill to the parking lot, do you recall if any of your friends carried anything in their hands?"

"I think so, yeah."

"Did Andreas carry anything? And if so, what was it?"

"Yes, I think he had a stick."

"Was there use of any sticks when you got to the parking lot?"

"No."

"What did you observe when you got up the hill to the parking lot?"

"I saw two cars with Cambridge kids take off outta the parking lot."

"Did anyone remain after those cars left?"

"Yes, there were some other Cambridge kids—four, I think—that stayed in the parking lot."

"What happened next?"

"A police car pulled into the parking lot, so we all ran."

"Where did you go?"

"We ran back down the same hill we'd come up, then we cut across the golf course over to the left side of the fairway toward the first hole."

"And then what happened?"

"I went back up the hill to see if anything was goin' on. I saw a police cruiser, so I ran back down the hill and told everyone there was a cop car in the parking lot at the top of the hill. So we just sat down on the golf course and talked for about ten minutes or so."

"After that, did anyone go back up the hill?"

"Yes, I did with Randy Harvey."

"What did you observe from your vantage point at the top of the hill?"

"I saw four Cambridge kids walkin' down Grove Street. They turned onto Huron Avenue and started walkin' toward us. Then they stopped where our cars were parked at the side of the road. One of them opened up the doors to both cars and looked inside."

"What did those four individuals do after they looked in the cars?"

"They just kept walkin' down Huron Avenue toward Glacken Field."

"And then what happened?"

"A white car turned off Grove Street and went past me on Huron Avenue. When it stopped by the four kids, I yelled to my friends in the golf course that the Cambridge kids were up the hill. At that time, everyone ran up from the golf course and out onto Huron Avenue."

"What happened next?"

"As we started to run toward the kids, they all jumped into a white car and took off down Huron Avenue toward Cambridge," Brian responded. "We started walkin' back up the road to our cars. Then we just stood around the cars talkin'. We weren't really doin' anything, for, I don't know, ten, maybe fifteen, minutes. While we were standin' there, we noticed a white car comin' up Huron Avenue toward Belmont. But then it stopped about halfway, made a U-turn, went back down Huron Avenue toward Cambridge, and went around the corner. Once it was out of our sight, we turned back around and saw a mess of kids comin' up Huron Avenue toward us."

"Now when you say, 'a mess of kids,' can you tell us how many you mean?" Mr. Rapacki questioned.

"At least thirty."

"And do you recall whether or not they had anything in their hands?"

"Yeah. They had sticks and bats."

"And what did you do when you saw these thirty or so kids coming up Huron Avenue?"

"We just stayed at our cars at first while they kept walkin'. Then a police car pulled up right behind them and started followin' them up the road."

Please officer, turn on your flashing lights and stop your cruiser! Park your cruiser sideways in the middle of the street and create distance between these two groups of boys. You can stop this. Please, please, please do something to stop this!

"So we just stood in the middle of the street, kinda spread out. We didn't walk forward or anything. We just stood where we were. But the Cambridge kids kept walkin' toward us."

Shortly after the murder and well before the trial, Brian had told me he thought they were safe because the police were there.

"Where did the police cruiser go?" Mr. Rapacki continued.

"It followed them for a while, then it drove past us, so I'm not sure. I think maybe it turned left onto Grove Street."

"At that point, did you turn to look at the group of kids who were walking toward you?"

"Yes."

"Approximately how close were they to you by then?"

"I'd say approximately eighty to ninety feet."

"And then what did you observe?"

"We just stayed there while they kept walkin' toward us. The next thing I knew, they were about ten feet away."

"When the groups were ten feet apart, what happened?"

"I noticed one of the Cambridge kids walkin' toward the side of the road, almost like he was tryin' to walk up behind us," Brian answered.

"And where did that person go?"

"When he got about right next to me, I turned and said, 'Where the hell do you think you're goin', you little shit?'"

"And did he respond?"

"No, he just stopped in his tracks and put one of his hands down in front of his pants."

"Your Honor, permission for the witness to step down and demonstrate for the jury the movements of the person he's describing?" Mr. Rapacki requested.

"Permission granted, but he can just stand up and demonstrate right there," the judge acknowledged.

"When I said somethin' to him again, he just stood there like this," Brian said as he rose to show the jury how the young man had stood with his legs spread out a bit. "Then he put his hand down his pants, like this," Brian continued, moving his right hand down to his waistline.

"Can you describe the person who you observed in that position?" Mr. Rapacki asked.

"Kinda small—smaller than me, I mean. The only other thing I really remember about him was that he had really short hair, like a flattop."

"Was this person white or black?"

"White."

"Now, at that point, were you able to observe where Andreas was?"

"No, I wasn't."

"What happened next?"

"After I said somethin' to the guy, I just stood there lookin' at him for a couple seconds, and then some words were exchanged, you know, 'What do you guys want? Why are you startin' this?' I don't know who said what, but all of a sudden, a tall, skinny kid came from the middle of the pack, right up to our friend Randy Harvey. Then he just punched Randy right in the face."

"And then what happened?"

"A big brawl started. Everyone just started fightin'."

"And what did you do?" Mr. Rapacki continued.

"Just as I turned, I noticed two people in front of me; one was holdin' a broomstick and the other was just, like, jumpin' around."

"So what did you do?"

"I just put up my hands as he swung the stick at me, you know, to block it with my arms. Then they started to chase me. I thought my arm was broken, so I kinda just ran around the corner of Grove Street. They didn't follow me, so I checked out my arm to make sure it was alright. It seemed to be OK, so I headed back to Huron Avenue."

Brian's testimony was an assault on my senses. My mind spun with the images his detailed answers created. Knowing what would come next, I wanted to press my palms tightly against my ears and block out all sound, but instead, I began silently repeating, like a mantra, *Please make the cruiser come back. Please make the cruiser come back. Please make the cruiser come back.* With an altered sense of time and place, I made my silent plea to the driverless cruiser. My mind only returned to the proceedings when I heard Mr. Rapacki say, "Your Honor, I have no further questions for Mr. Walsh at this time."

The defense attorney stood up and shuffled to the podium as if buying himself a bit of extra time to think. Then he began his cross-examination. "OK, Brian, so when these thirty young men came up Huron Avenue, you could see that some of them were armed. Is that correct?" the defense attorney asked assertively.

"Yes, sir."

"And they were carrying sticks, bats, and broomsticks, right?"

"Yes."

"And hockey sticks?"

"Yeah, I guess so," Brian replied. "They were all holdin' sticks and bats and things like that."

"And you got hit with one, right?"

"Yes, sir."

Lucy had been watching me hold back tears and motioned for me to leave the courtroom with her. A compassionate woman, she nonetheless needed to ensure that I would not begin to cry or react in some other way that might influence the jury and hurt the prosecution. *Has she noticed that I'm losing strength?* I wondered.

Outside in the quiet corridor, I blurted out, "I can't stand that defense attorney! He's like a devil!" Standing reassuringly close to me, Lucy looked me straight in the eye. "His role is to challenge and poke holes in the prosecution's theory of the murder," she explained, her voice firm yet kind. "It's all about planting a seed of reasonable doubt in the jury's mind."

"Do you see how the lawyer keeps putting his arm around the murderer?"

"Remember Christine, the defendant is considered innocent until proven guilty beyond a reasonable doubt. He is entitled to a defense."

I listened to her explanations in silence and began to breathe deeply. Lucy was a grounding presence, and together we returned to the courtroom. I needed to be there for Andreas.

The defense attorney was still cross-examining Brian when we reached our seats. *That's his job*, I kept repeating to myself. *Just sit there and let yourself hear what he has to say*, I reminded myself. Finally, the defense attorney returned to his place next to the defendant and the trial was over for the day. As the bailiff called out, "All rise," I was surprised that my legs could still hold me.

—⟋⟋⟍—

Robert and I drove home along busy Cambridge streets in silence, still shocked after another agonizing day spent listening to witness testimony at the trial. At the house, I made sandwiches for the two of us, and then changed my clothes, reached for my bag with the note-book and pens, and headed over to the cemetery to be with my son. Today, especially, I needed to be with Andreas. I drove down Arling-ton Street and through the back entrance of Mount Auburn Cemetery. Knowing I could sit with him in silence among the trees beneath the wide-open sky gave me solace.

Monday, October 2, 1989
My dear Andreas,
I survived another day listening to witnesses. My heart bleeds nonstop knowing how naive you and your friends were that night. You went to show guys you didn't even know that you weren't afraid. I simply cannot comprehend that. Didn't you have better things to do? Shortly before you were born, we moved to Belmont so you and Tom could grow up in a safe place.

Andreas, today I constantly wished to rewind the tape. If only one of you had expressed some doubts before the attack, the evening would've had a very different ending and you would still be with us. Instead, I write this as I sit next to your grave.

Andreas, the horror of your death still shakes my whole being. I can't believe you will never come home again. It's incomprehensible to me. I'm having strong yearnings to come join you, but I can't leave Tom behind.

I miss you so much—more than words can say. Your absence has left a blunt, never-ending pain in my heart. I fear tomorrow.

I don't know whether I can stand being in the same room with your accused murderer and his attorneys for another day.

My dear son, I love you forever.

With a shattered heart,

Mom

CHAPTER 11

Day Four

I can't go back there again. I dragged myself from room to room, trying to ready myself for yet another day in court. It was Tuesday, October 3—day four of the trial—and I dressed slowly, putting on my brown pants and an off-white blouse as Robert finished up in the bathroom.

A little while later, as we drove to the courthouse in silence, I said to Robert in a shaky voice, "I can't do this anymore." When his face turned stern, I immediately realized I should not have said anything. He needed me to remain strong.

We knew we had an exceedingly difficult day ahead of us. *What's it going to be like to see the surgeon on the witness stand? Will I be able to hold back my tears while he describes how he tried to save Andreas's life? I don't want to prejudice the jury. I don't want the judge to declare a mistrial because of my tears. But will I be able to sit there quietly and listen to the exact details of Andreas's injuries—how big the knife wound was—without breaking down? Mike will testify today too. I'll definitely be in the courtroom when he takes the stand, but I'll have to be careful about how much I let myself hear. I can't go in there anymore and have my gaze pulled in the direction of the accused and see his attorneys' arms around his shoulders.*

Despite my internal struggle, the car rolled on in the direction of the courthouse. Soon, Robert and I were sitting in our regular places on the courtroom bench next to Lucy. *How is it that this bench is becoming harder and more uncomfortable each day? My body aches. I'm exhausted and weak. Oh, how I wish I could sink deeply into a soft-cushioned chair for a bit of comfort.* After the intensity of the past three days, I felt emotionally and physically drained. My body and soul had already absorbed too many excruciating details of Andreas's suffering, images that would stay with me—together with his sweet smile and gentle heart—until the end of my days. Robert, Lucy, and the parents of Andreas's friends appeared like a fog that surrounded me.

As the trial resumed, I shifted my attention to the witness stand. I recognized the doctor who had operated on Andreas the night of the attack, although he looked different dressed in a dark suit and tie rather than the white coat he wore over his surgical scrubs when I'd last seen him. The start of the soft-spoken doctor's testimony took me back to the night Andreas lay dying in the hospital room, accompanied only by medical staff as Robert and I waited, huddled together in another room as instructed. Throughout that night of waiting, the surgeon had kept us informed. He came once to tell us how the surgery went and of his hope that Andreas's body temperature, which was extremely low, would rise. I kept praying to God to keep Andreas alive, but with each short visit, the doctor's reports became more dire. "His temperature is not coming up. If he survives, he will need a liver transplant."

Mike's mother, Maureen, who was a nurse, sat with us during some of that seemingly endless night. I felt a little comfort as she told us that her aunt in Ireland was praying for us and for Andreas. *Will the doctor come and tell us that Andreas is OK? Can we see him now? Where is Tom? Is he with Andreas's friends? I hope Tom is not alone.*

I would learn from Tom many years later that he was, in fact, utterly alone for most of that night, sitting in a cubicle by himself, right next to where he could hear the medical staff frantically trying to save his brother's life. In our confusion and terror, Robert and I had assumed Tom was with Andreas's friends and their parents in the waiting room, anticipating news of Andreas's condition. To this day, that experience continues to haunt Tom as he remembers the nurses yelling, "It's the wrong blood type! It's the wrong blood!"

A barrage of sounds and images assaulted my senses as the attorney continued to question the surgeon. The doctor answered each question in unspeakable detail, quite matter-of-factly and clinically stating the type and extent of Andreas's injuries. Seeing the defendant sitting not far from where I sat between Robert and Lucy brought me back to the present, to the reality of being in the courtroom mere yards from the person accused of taking Andreas's life. *I'm not in the emergency room. The doctor can no longer save Andreas.*

Suddenly, the wooden bench beneath me and the whole room began to spin out of control as the doctor continued to recount the injuries Andreas had sustained. Lucy whispered in my ear, "Christine, do you want to go out into the hallway?"

I nodded my head and then fled the room with her, my legs barely able to keep my body upright.

Once we were outside the courtroom, Lucy asked, "Are you alright?"

Shaking my head, I said, "I can't listen to another word of what the doctor says."

"Why don't you stay out here for a while and take a break. It's OK not to listen to everything said," Lucy assured me. "It must be very difficult to see Andreas's doctor." Then she returned to the courtroom.

Relieved to be out of the courtroom, I began to pace slowly up and down the hallway, trying to calm myself by concentrating on my breath and the sensation of my feet touching the concrete floor. Looking up, I saw a tall young man, about the same height as Andreas, across from me. For a split second, a spark of joy entered my heart. *It's Mike! If he's here, Andreas must be nearby.*

I approached Andreas's longtime friend and reached my arms toward him as I said, "How are you doing? How are you holding up, Mike?"

As I reached up to give him a hug, he bent down toward me a bit to equalize our heights, just as Andreas used to do. Mike hesitated for a moment before responding, "I'm OK."

We looked at each other as if noticing that we'd both changed. To me, he'd become a surviving link to my son's short life. To him, I'd become the mother of his murdered friend. *How does one relate to her? Is that what he's wondering?*

"I've been thinkin' back to the time when we went to the Bahamas with Andreas," Mike told me, the words cascading out of his mouth. "That was such a fun time! Andreas loved ridin' motorbikes all around the island and swimmin' in the warm ocean water."

Andreas lives! How normal that felt. I smiled at Mike, thanking him for the gift of a precious memory.

But Mike did not return my smile. Instead, his face became very serious. Just above a whisper, he said, "Don, our friend from school, committed suicide. They found him yesterday in his car. He was at Andreas's funeral. He said then that when he dies, he wants a burial like Andreas's."

I trembled as I recalled Don as a boy, perhaps twelve or thirteen years old, standing on our back steps clutching a basketball under his right arm. "Is Andreas home?" he'd asked as I'd opened the door, his jet-black hair shining in the sunlight. I thought of how I'd watched Don and Andreas walk away from the house that day, bouncing the ball as they approached the nearby playground. *Was that really only six or seven years ago?* Now both Don and Andreas were gone.

"How horribly sad. I'm so sorry, Mike," I replied, shaking my head at this tragic news.

When it was Mike's turn to testify, I returned to the courtroom. I didn't want to miss a word of what he had to say.

"How old are you, Mr. Driscoll?" Mr. Rapacki asked.

"I'm nineteen," Mike replied.

"Do you go to school?"

"Yes, I do. I'm a sophomore in college."

"How long have you—had you—known Andreas?"

"I'm not sure of the grade, but we met in elementary school in either second or third grade."

Hearing Mike mention how long he and Andreas had known one another triggered a memory of a conversation I'd had with Mike not long before the trial began. "Andreas and I became inseparable," he'd said, "'cause students were always arranged alphabetically by last name, so Driscoll and Dresp were always together."

My thoughts returned to the present as Mike continued to answer Mr. Rapacki's questions. "After we got to Glacken Field, me and my friends felt very uncomfortable there 'cause some Cambridge kids were sayin', 'Where's your passes? What are you guys doin' here?' So we all decided to leave."

"Where did you go?"

"We headed to the parking lot. I was trailin' about a hundred feet behind, and when I got to my car, my friend Tim Killilea was in an argument with a boy with a bat."

"What happened when you saw Tim Killilea in an argument with the boy with the bat?"

"I walked up behind the guy, tapped him on the shoulder, and said, 'Look, if you wanna fight, put the bat down. And if you wanna get a few of your friends, fine. But we don't wanna fight, we just wanna leave.'"

"How long were you with the guy with the bat?"

"Just a few minutes. Then he got another friend, a short guy. But then he ran and got a whole group of friends. I'm not sure how many exactly, but I'd say between thirty and forty. So we just said, 'Forget this,' and we got in our car and left."

"And where did you go?"

"To Andreas's house. We were all extremely mad about the situation. We knew about another party in Belmont where some of our other friends were, so me, Todd, and Jeff Taylor went to that party and told our friends about what had happened."

"Now, prior to leaving Andreas's house, do you recall people locating some sticks."

"Yeah, I do. I'm not sure who grabbed them, though. I just remember that we opened up the garage and some of the guys grabbed a broken broom and a broken-off hockey stick that we used to play stickball."

"When you went to the party in Belmont, who stayed behind?"

"It was Eric, Andreas, and Tim."

"When you returned to the scene, to the intersection of Huron and Grove, how many friends from the party came back with you?"

"I don't remember exactly, but I think there were seven or eight that came from the party."

"And where did you guys go?"

"We parked the cars down at the bottom of the intersection, then we walked up through the golf course to Glacken Field."

"What happened next?"

"We came around by the clubhouse, and there were about twenty or thirty Cambridge kids there. Most of them ran off, but a few stayed, and we talked to them. And, for the most part, I thought we'd straightened everything out. Then a police cruiser came by, and everybody ran down the hill toward the entrance to the golf course. We were ready to go home, but this white car kept drivin' by and the people inside it were yellin' stuff. We were a little reluctant to leave, so we just stood at the bottom of the hill by the cars."

"And this is on Huron Avenue, correct?"

"Yes."

"What did you see there?"

"The white car drove by again, and it was weird. All of a sudden, a bunch of kids just came outta nowhere."

"How many were there?"

"I'd say twenty-five to thirty. And they all looked like they had somethin' in their hands. I'd had a broken-off broomstick, but I dropped it when the police came, so I was a little scared. And at that time, half my friends were across the street in Grove Street Park or by the cars."

"Do you recall who was at Grove Street Park?"

"I don't. I just know that Randy Harvey was with me when the Cambridge kids were comin' at us."

"And what happened when the Cambridge kids came down the hill?" Mr. Rapacki asked.

"Well, as far as I remember, there was a cruiser in the cemetery and a cruiser right next to the kids as they were makin' their way down the street, and I was thinkin' that unless the cops were crazy, they were gonna stop the kids 'cause it seemed like they all had somethin' in their hands. So I was kinda worried, but I also wasn't 'cause the cops were right there. Me and Randy just stood there when the kids came down. And when the first punch was thrown, it was from a kid who hit Randy."

"And where was the police cruiser at this point?"

"It was behind the kids from Cambridge, like at an angle. When the kids got to us, it seemed like the cruiser stopped short."

Why did the police do nothing? Why didn't they stop the attacking crowd?

"What happened after Randy Harvey was punched?"

"He fell forward, and I was a little shocked 'cause I'd never seen anyone get hit that hard. After that, I remember fightin' with one or two kids. Then I got hit in the back with somethin', and I fell down. As I was rollin' around in pain, I got kicked and hit a few times, so I stood up. But I was still in shock, so I started backin' up a little. Then I looked to my left when I heard Andreas screamin'."

"When you heard Andreas screaming and looked to your left, what did you see?"

"I saw him just coated in blood. I ran over to him, and I was just in shock."

"Where was Andreas?"

"He was leanin' on a car."

"When you looked over and saw Andreas, did you see anybody else near him?"

"No."

"Now, Mr. Driscoll, at any time during the fight, prior to seeing Andreas leaning on a car, when was the last time that you saw him?"

"I don't remember seein' him during the fight at all—just after I heard him scream."

"I have no further questions, Your Honor," Mr. Rapacki said.

"Any cross-examination?" the judge asked.

"Yes, Your Honor, briefly," Mr. Harris replied.

The defense attorney interrogated Mike in such a way that it was obvious—at least to me—that he was trying to poke holes in Mike's testimony and the statements that he'd given to police. Mr. Harris seemed to focus on the fact that Mike had told the police that he'd witnessed two black men running away from the scene, so his line of questioning intimated that it could've been one of these two men who stabbed Andreas. But Mike wasn't going to let the defense attorney put words into his mouth. He was adamant that, although two black men were running away from the scene, they were not running away from Andreas.

After another grueling day in court, Robert and I drove home. The repeated exposure to the grisly details of my child's death had left me in a state of shock. "I heard him scream," Mike had testified. His words reverberated throughout my body.

It was late afternoon when I got back into my car and sought solace in the only place I could—at the cemetery. By the earthy, narrow path to Andreas's grave, I was struck by the changing color of the katsura trees. As I looked up to take in the buttery yellow of the early fall leaves, a cool breeze blew against my tear-drenched face. I walked slowly toward the two old pine trees that had stood guard near Andreas's grass-covered grave since the day he was buried. Sturdy and deeply rooted in the earth, they stood tall and unmoving despite the light wind. In sadness and rage, I thought, *They're older than Andreas, and yet they're still here!*

The stillness of the empty cemetery enveloped me. Suddenly, as if a river dam had failed, a powerful rage flowed through me like uncontrolled, roiling water. I stomped my feet and silently screamed, *Stop spinning, Earth! Fall off your axis! Can you at least acknowledge my pain? I want to die! Death, please take me! I can't bear anymore suffering!*

With my gaze fixed on Andreas's final resting place, which still didn't have a headstone, I spoke to him through my tears. "Andreas, I want to join you wherever you are. Being in this world without you has no meaning anymore. Where are you? Where did you go?" At that moment, a warm breeze caressed my cheeks. I turned my face up toward the overcast sky and a supplicating voice from within me asked, *Andreas, is that you? Are you the warm breeze letting me know you're here?*

CHAPTER 12

Day Five

O n the fifth day of the trial, Robert and I left home as if going to the courthouse had become our new routine, part of our everyday lives. For a moment, I even felt a glimpse of being normal again, like the two of us were simply going out to an early breakfast at our neighborhood diner while our sons were away at college.

At the courthouse, we had to drive up to the garage's rooftop to find a place to park. After leaving our car, I kept turning my head to make sure nobody was following us. My heart pounded in my chest like a beating drum as I descended the narrow staircase. A bitter autumn wind cut through us as we trudged down the sidewalk of the busy street. *Should I not go inside, just let the unforgiving wind blow me backward? I really don't want to go in there.*

I knew that we were going to hear testimony from some of the defendant's friends. I also knew we'd hear details from the medical examiner, the crime laboratory chemist, a detective, and a fingerprint expert. Lucy had warned us that photos of Andreas's dead body would be shown to the lawyers and jurors. Knowing I had not been able to comfort him or at least stand by him as he took his last breaths, I couldn't bear to look at the photos. I longed for everyone in the courtroom to see photos of Andreas as he was in life. I still hoped Andreas might be making the drive from UMass Lowell and would soon walk through our door, his green duffel bag thrown over one shoulder as he had done not so long ago.

Five days in, Robert and I went straight to Courtroom B on the sixth floor, no longer waiting for Lucy to accompany us. We knew she would join us before the proceedings began. Unlike the first few days of the trial, my body no longer felt like it was floating. *Have I become used to walking by the defendant's mother on our way to our seats on the other side of the wooden bench?* Throughout the trial, Lucy had been the only partition between us.

The multiplicity of my feelings, the images within me, and the sounds I'd heard during the past few days of testimony instantly rose to the surface as the actors appeared once again on the stage. Soon the familiar "All rise!" announced the continuation of the trial and, with that, additional witnesses were called to the stand. I listened as scenes of the street fight and the attack on Andreas were described in shocking detail. Images of his blood flowing out onto the street and the size and depth of the knife wound crushed my already heavy heart. I blinked back tears. *Keep swallowing. Don't let any teardrops fall*, I kept thinking to myself, tightening all my muscles so as not to let out a shriek. The thought of the speed and force the killer used to cut through Andreas's young skin sickened me and stiffened my body.

"Christine, do you want to leave the room?" Lucy asked in a whisper.

I shook my head and sat rooted to the bench. I watched the murderer's hand fly toward Andreas. I saw my son's blood seep through his neatly pressed shirt and quickly spread. I heard the sickening crack of the stick as it hit his skull.

"Christine, how about taking a little break. Let's go outside," Lucy repeated, this time directing me rather than asking a question.

Once outside the courtroom, in the windowless hallway, my body came to a standstill. "Christine, you needed a break. I was worried you would start crying. The judge is strict about any show of emotion," Lucy warned.

I looked fixedly at her moving lips. "Stop the trial because of people showing their emotions? You mean he could declare a mistrial because of *that*, and the defendant would walk out of here a free man?"

"Yes," Lucy replied resolutely. "You must understand, by exposing the jurors to your intense feelings, they might lose their objectivity. The decision of guilt beyond a reasonable doubt must not be colored by the jurors' emotional reactions to the intensity of the victim's pain nor to the pain of his loved ones. They might feel pressured to find the defendant guilty just to please you. It's called prejudicing the jury."

"Isn't the defendant prejudicing the jury every single day we're here in court? He sits there in full view of the jury, almost right next to them. Doesn't his sad demeanor and his young body in his oversize suit prejudice the jury?"

"That's different. It shows them who he is."

"What about who *Andreas was*? When do they get to see or hear that?" I exclaimed. "I don't understand. How about when the lawyers put their arms around the defendant's shoulders and whisper into his ear? Won't the jurors pity him and be prejudiced in that way? Because they get to know him, won't it be difficult for them to imagine him killing my son? Won't it be difficult for them to find him guilty? Even *I* feel sorry for him. If I were a juror, I don't know if I could send him to jail for life," I said angrily as Lucy listened attentively.

"It goes back to this being a defendant-oriented legal process."

"It's not fair that if I shed a tear while sitting in there listening to everything my son had to endure that I risk making the trial invalid. It's not fair!" I vented to Lucy. "In the hospital, we weren't allowed to see Andreas. They had to keep him attached to the machines for the coroner. The legal concerns took precedence over our emotional needs as his family. We couldn't even say goodbye."

A stream of pent-up frustration fell as tears against my cheeks as Lucy gently touched my arm and said, "Christine, why don't you stay out here for a little while, and I'll go in and see how Robert is doing."

A few minutes later, Lucy returned with Robert. Together, the three of us stood motionless. Nervously, Lucy said, "The judge just threatened to stop the trial. Some of the parents of Andreas's friends burst out crying." Robert stared straight ahead, barely blinking.

After sharing this unsettling update, Robert and Lucy went back inside the courtroom. I needed a few more minutes alone to collect myself. Before long, Lucy returned to escort me back in. As I followed her to my seat beside my husband, I could sense how dense the atmosphere in the room had become. It was as if an unseen, yet palpable, fog had engulfed the courtroom, absorbing all sound. Despite the brief corridor breaks I had taken throughout the day, the abhorrent images conjured up by the parade of medical and forensic experts had left me gasping for air. I heard only my own labored breathing. *I can't hold up any longer. But I need to stay for Andreas.*

Mercifully, the bailiff's voice soon echoed throughout the room, "All rise!" Clearly the judge had called for the court to adjourn for the day, but I didn't hear him. I began to breathe more easily once I heard people shifting their weight from one foot to the other and saw the somber jurors shuffling out of the room. Lucy and Robert stood close to me in silence.

"Tomorrow, each lawyer will present his closing argument, and then the case will go to the jury for deliberation," Lucy said while we waited for the defendant's supporters to leave the room.

What if the jurors don't find him guilty? What if they feel they haven't seen enough evidence to sentence him to life in prison? Will he just walk out alongside us a free man, while Andreas remains gone forever?

Robert stepped forward to speak to Mr. Rapacki. "How do you see the case going?" he asked.

"It went as well as it could. The witnesses did a good job. I hope the jury heard what they said, but there are no guarantees. You never know how juries think. I'll do my best tomorrow to convince the jurors that the evidence shows he's the one. Then we just have to wait and see what they decide."

After listening intently to Mr. Rapacki's words, Robert said, "Thank you for the job you've done. We'll see you tomorrow."

—∿—

On that crisp autumn day, as I did every day after attending the trial, I had the urge to be with Andreas. At the cemetery, I tended to the flowers on his grave before sitting down to write:

Wednesday, October 4, 1989
Dear Andreas,
Your dad and I spent most of today in court. It was the fifth day of the trial, and I'm barely hanging on. Now I just need to be with you here at the cemetery. The pink asters in the pot here look more beautiful each day. Julia's bouquet of yellow mums and orange lilies still brighten your resting place. When I arrived today, I saw that somebody had added a large bouquet of peach-colored dahlias and dark purple zinnias, the kind you would've loved to see in our home. The bouquet has no card, but surely it shows much love for you and us as a family. It comforts me that you haven't been forgotten.

Some people have placed pumpkins on nearby graves. When I look at them, I picture you and Tom trick-or-treating, but I can't remember what Halloween costumes you wore. Did you ever go as Batman and Tom as Robin? On second thought, I'm pretty sure it was the reverse: you were Robin and Tom was Batman.

Andreas, the summer has disappeared. I can't bear to think that with the change of seasons, you'll be left behind. I don't know how to go on.

Witness testimony ended today. Tomorrow morning, attorneys for the defense and the prosecution will present their closing arguments, and then the jury will go into a special room to decide what the verdict will be. The accused could get first-degree or second-degree murder, or he could walk out of the courtroom a free man. Whatever happens to him, it won't bring you back, but at least if he goes to prison, he won't be able to kill anyone else and destroy another family.

Andreas, although it's only been a few months since it was planted from seed, the grass that covers you now is full and lush. Above you, sunlight streams through rustling leaves, creating a dance of light and shadow that I know you would love.

I miss you more than I miss anyone else on this earth.
I will always love you,
Your broken mom

CHAPTER 13

Day Six

Thursday, October 5, was the sixth day of the trial. Robert drove to the courthouse as if on autopilot. Once inside, the pounding of my heart mingled with the clacking of footsteps moving across the lobby. While waiting for the elevator door to slide open, I kept my head still, but my eyes darted from side to side, trying to see who was standing next to me. I feared it was "them," the supporters of the accused. *Just remain calm,* I told myself. Robert, presumably immersed in his own fears, stared blankly ahead as the elevator door opened.

When Robert and I took our seats at the end of the bench, the defendant and his team were sitting at their table. The mother of the accused had not yet arrived. There was an empty space among the women where his mother usually sat.

Soon, Lucy joined us. Djano and another of Andreas's friends from high school sat in the last row behind the parents, their ashen faces devoid of the carefree smiles they wore just a few months earlier. *Will the jurors reach a verdict today? Will the accused walk out a free man? Will today be the last day? Please let this end.*

I noticed some movement on the other side of the bench and realized that the defendant's mother and some other women were taking their seats. Immediately, the bailiff called out, "All rise," as if he'd been waiting for them to arrive.

"Good morning, ladies and gentlemen," the judge said in his usual calm manner as he addressed the jury. "Let me remind you that closing arguments are not evidence. They are an opportunity for the attorneys, depending on their point of view, to either tear apart or put together the case, to ask you *not* to draw conclusions or ask you *to* draw conclusions.

"Now, you won't hear from either of these two experienced attorneys anything like, "I believe that" or "I don't believe such-and-such witness" because lawyers are not permitted to present their personal views or endorsements. They may certainly argue to you that the evidence shows something or that it doesn't, but they may not offer their own views of a witness's credibility or lack of credibility." After speaking directly to the jury, the judge turned his attention to the defendant's lead attorney and said, "You may proceed, Mr. Harris."

This means the defense attorney has one more chance to plead for the defendant's life. He'll argue that his client is innocent, and that the prosecution failed to prove its case. How can the jury think this defendant, who looks so young in his oversize suit, could be capable of such an atrocious act?

The defense attorney slowly lifted his body from the chair, flipped open the button of his dark suit jacket, and stepped away from his client. The defendant leaned his body toward the remaining attorney, who placed his right arm on his client's shoulder. At the podium, Mr. Harris looked straight at the jurors and began to speak.

"This is the defense's closing argument," he said. "It's an opportunity to argue the evidence in the case. Mr. Rapacki will argue the evidence for the Commonwealth last; he'll have the last word between the parties. That's an advantage, members of the jury, an advantage the Commonwealth enjoys because they bear the burden of proof. And it's a heavy burden to prove something beyond a reasonable doubt, to a moral certainty, so I ask you to recognize that burden and hold the Commonwealth to it.

"Members of the jury, when you deliberate, ask yourselves: what evidence did the Commonwealth produce to prove beyond a reasonable doubt that Corey McCale murdered Andreas Dresp? There's no disputing the fact that Andreas is dead, and that's a tragedy. No one should suffer an untimely death; no one should suffer the physical harm and injury that Andreas suffered; and no family should go through what his family is going through. But don't compound the tragedy, don't double the wrong. Don't convict a man of a crime that he didn't commit."

Could Mr. Harris be right? I contemplated. *I believe the prosecution has demonstrated through witness testimony that Corey McCale alone is responsible for Andreas's death. But what if he didn't do it? What if the defense attorney is right?*

"He didn't have a stick. He didn't hit the young man on the head with a bat. And he didn't stab him. The Commonwealth can't prove something that didn't happen.

"Members of the jury, my client pleaded not guilty because he is innocent. He knew that the day he entered his plea, and he knows that today as he sits here before you. Corey McCale has always maintained his innocence, and he will continue to do so for the rest of his life because he did not commit this crime. Members of the jury, I ask you to take the law into the deliberation room and apply it to the facts of the case as you find them, then return to this courtroom with the only reasonable verdict in the case: not guilty. Thank you."

Lucy stayed close as we left the courtroom together for a short break. I watched Robert as he came to stand stiffly next to one wall of the corridor, his face colorless as if drained of all life. Lucy looked at us with a serious expression and said, "Remember, it's his job to defend his client. What he just said isn't evidence; it's just his point of view. The jurors will look at the evidence."

Too soon, Robert and I found ourselves back on our bench in the courtroom to hear the prosecutor's closing argument. "Good morning, ladies and gentlemen," Mr. Rapacki said from the podium. He leaned forward a bit and looked directly at the jurors. "When I gave my opening statement, I told you the Commonwealth wouldn't prove that somebody saw the stabbing nor would the Commonwealth present a witness who said, 'I saw what happened.' I also said the Commonwealth *would* prove to you—beyond a reasonable doubt—that the defendant, Corey McCale, committed this murder.

"Now perhaps the best witness of all is one you didn't hear from, at least not verbally, and that's Andreas. It would be wonderful for everybody if Andreas were here to tell us what happened to him. But he's not because he's dead. He's not coming back. But in death, Andreas provided us—provided you—with the most important evidence that you'll consider during your deliberations: He gave you himself, ladies and gentlemen. He gave you his blood. He gave you the wound on his body, the damage to his liver.

"As I go through the testimony, I'll refer back to that critical evidence Andreas left behind, and I urge you to think about it as you put the pieces of the puzzle together and see how Andreas, even in death, is your most important witness."

Andreas lives! Mr. Rapacki keeps mentioning his name.

"Ladies and gentlemen, what does Andreas tell us? What does Andreas leave for us to see? One stab wound—one five-centimeter-long stab wound on the right side of his body. Only one person could've stabbed Andreas, and only one person did stab Andreas."

Hearing Mr. Rapacki repeat Andreas's name over and over, I began to feel deep gratitude for him: gratitude for humanizing my son and showing the suffering he endured. At moments, his words seemed enveloped in a brightness that stirred a warm breeze in the dark place inside my heart. *Andreas, are you here with me? Are you the breeze?*

"Only one person killed Andreas Dresp, ladies and gentlemen, and it's the defendant, Corey McCale. Once you reach that conclusion, however, your task is not yet complete. Having concluded that the defendant murdered Andreas Dresp, you have to decide whether it was first- or second-degree murder. It's murder because he used a knife. First-degree murder means it was premeditated, *deliberately* premeditated. Listen closely to His Honor's definition of what that means, then think about what the defendant did, how he took the knife and thrust the blade into Andreas deeper and deeper until it couldn't go any further. That knife didn't get there by accident, ladies and gentlemen, and it didn't get pushed in all the way without somebody thinking and wanting it to go in all the way.

"And then what did the defendant do? He punched Andreas. And why did he punch Andreas? Because the knife was broken. He couldn't use it anymore, and Andreas was still wrestling with his friend Kevin Smith, so Mr. McCale picked up the stick and hit Andreas twice to finish him off.

"If you truly have a reasonable doubt as to whether or not it was the defendant who killed Andreas Dresp, then you should return a verdict of not guilty. But there is no such doubt, so you must have the courage to return the only true verdict: guilty of murder in the first degree. Thank you, ladies and gentlemen."

As Mr. Rapacki returned to his seat, a powerful silence fell over the courtroom. From the moment Andreas's friends had arrived at our home that fateful night in June, wild-eyed and breathless and crying out, "Andreas was hurt in a fight," I had been in a state of disbelief. But now, with the prosecutor's final words, any shred of sensing, of wishing, of hoping to find Andreas safely in his bedroom at the end of this nightmare, was forever extinguished.

"Members of the jury, you are about to decide this case. You must do so without fear, favor, bias, partiality, or sympathy toward anyone," the judge instructed. "As I've said, your job is to decide the facts. Your vote must be unanimous—all twelve of you must agree—so take as much time as you need."

What's happening in the jurors' box? Is there some kind of lottery taking place?

"The jury's being reduced to twelve," Lucy whispered into my ear as if she'd heard my internal thoughts. "These twelve will reach a verdict. The others are alternates."

As the jurors stood up to leave the room, I couldn't help but think, *They're carrying so much responsibility! Andreas, please be with the jurors and let your spirit's presence support them in this difficult job.*

These men and women who don't even know us have allowed themselves to witness the horror of my son's death. The jurors will now decide whether the accused will walk out alongside us as a free man or whether he'll be placed behind bars and barbed wire.

I wanted neither option for this young man, but I needed to have the person who killed Andreas locked up. I needed to be able to stop looking over my shoulder and know that my family and friends could again go to the grocery store or to the cemetery without worrying that the murderer might find one of us. I also knew he had to be punished and face consequences so that he'd never kill someone else.

We remained standing at our seats while the defendant and his family and friends began walking toward the door. While we waited for them to leave, Lucy, with urgency in her normally calm voice, informed us, "You need to stay close to the courtroom so you can hear when they announce that the jury has reached a verdict. It can happen very quickly, or it might take a few hours or even days for the jury to reach a unanimous decision." As we made our way out of the courtroom, Lucy continued, "The judge won't accept a verdict between one and two, so you can go get something to eat during that time."

Robert and I took the elevator down to the cafeteria, which was crowded with men and women eating lunch at small tables. While waiting in line to order food, my eyes scanned the menu board but couldn't make sense of the words. Mike's mother approached us and anxiously exclaimed, "The defendant's family and supporters are all here! Let's go to a restaurant. There are several just down the street."

"I don't want to stay here either. Let's get out of here," I said to Robert.

But as we followed Mike's mother and the other parents of Andreas's friends, I worried that we might miss the verdict. In the noisy restaurant, the other parents talked, but I was too distracted to follow the conversation. *Are we missing the verdict?*

After lunch, Robert and I found ourselves back in the sunless corridor in front of Courtroom B. Robert seemed buried in his thoughts as I, lost in my own, began anxiously pacing back and forth.

The defendant's family and friends huddled together on their side of the corridor. Others sat on the cement steps of the back staircase, chain-smoking cigarettes and creating white spirals of smoke around them. A few women who also belonged to the "other side" stood at one end of the corridor, staring off into the distance. The defendant moved in and out of the various groups like a groom at a wedding reception.

It occurred to me that all of us were dreading the verdict but for different reasons. Something life-changing was being decided upon as we stood waiting in this sterile hallway, and none of us had any say in the outcome. We were all equally helpless and powerless as we let the process take its course. I stopped pacing and rejoined Robert. He stood very still at one end of the corridor, pensive with his sorrowful eyes downcast. As we waited for news from the courtroom, I was suddenly transported through time to that night in June. *Was it only four months ago that Robert, Tom, and I had waited together in the crowded emergency room?*

I thought of how stunned I'd been that night to see so many police officers comingling with Andreas's friends and some of their parents. My eyes, opened wide in fear and confusion, had scanned the ER. Leaning against the wall diagonally across from us were Brian, Mike, and Todd, who just hours before had stood in my kitchen, their shirts torn and hands shaking as they spewed out the words that had crushed my heart. Other friends sat on chairs, and one was lying on the floor, holding his head in his hands. All of them wore anxious expressions.

I vividly recalled a nurse appearing in the waiting area, glancing our way, and asking in a loud voice, "Are you the parents of Andreas Dresp?"

"Yes," Robert and I had answered resolutely, quickly peeling ourselves from the wall and turning toward the nurse.

"Please come with me," she'd said, letting the heavy door close behind us.

She's taking us to see Andreas! Where is he? I'd thought.

Robert had rushed toward an examining room and spoke fast as he asked the nurse repeatedly, "Where is Andreas? Where is he? We want to see him!"

"You can't go in there!" the nurse had bellowed as she placed her matronly body in front of us, blocking our path. "I thought he was going to die when he was wheeled in. His eyes had rolled back. The whole emergency room is closed to take care of your son. You have to wait outside!"

The force of her words had pushed us back into the waiting room where Brian, Todd, Mike, and some others were still leaning against the wall. I approached them, put my arms around Todd, and told the group what the nurse had said. Holding back tears, they'd said nothing, but I could see the apprehension, worry, and shock on their faces. I stumbled back to Robert and Tom, trapped fear hammering through my heart.

"We need to go back into the courtroom. It's five o'clock," Lucy said, interrupting my flashback of that horrific night.

Inside the courtroom, the judge rose to address the jurors. "Ladies and gentlemen, you've had a long day, so I'm going to send you home now. We'll reconvene at nine o'clock tomorrow morning."

After we set foot outside the building, I shook my head and thought, *Please let me wake up from this nightmare. Please!*

CHAPTER 14

Day Seven

Friday, October 6, marked the seventh day of the trial. It was Robert's birthday. After little sleep, nothing felt solid to me anymore. The many sounds I'd heard and images I'd seen during the previous six days in court had been permanently etched into my body and soul. *At least today I don't have to hear more details of how Andreas was killed.*

Before leaving for the courthouse, I placed birthday cards for Robert from his mother in New Jersey and my parents in Germany on our living room table and added my gifts. But I didn't feel like celebrating. Neither Tom nor Andreas was there to wish Robert a happy birthday and see him open his presents. When I placed a bouquet of pink roses on the table, I felt a hole in my chest. "It's 8:20," I said to Robert. "We have to leave now."

Will the jurors reach a verdict today? I wondered. "I hope this will be our last day in court," I remarked as Robert drove us to the courthouse.

"I hope so too," Robert replied, his eyes fixed on the road.

When we arrived at Courtroom B, as Robert, Lucy, and I sat in silence in our usual place on the bench, my body began to tremble. All I could think about was how soon we might have a verdict. Moments later, the jurors walked in to take their seats and the judge followed, his hands clasped in front of him pale against his black robe.

How close are they to making a decision? I thought. *Will they know how to arrive at an impartial decision based on the evidence? Please reach a just verdict, please. Be strong, don't give up!*

After a few encouraging words to the jury, the judge said, "Members of the jury, you may return to your deliberations."

My gaze followed the silent jurors as they left the courtroom. *Andreas, is your spirit with them?* It was 9:04 a.m.

—⟋⟍—

After the jury left the room to deliberate, the family and friends of the defendant exited the courtroom. Some leaned against the walls of the corridor, while others sat expressionless on the cement steps of the emergency exit staircase. A few women seemed contemplative, like nuns deep in prayer.

As Robert and I stood with the parents of Andreas's friends, I recognized that there were no exterior signals of the passing of time. We were suspended on the sixth floor of a square, concrete building, facing closed wooden doors and pacing the dim corridor. Again, the realization floated through my consciousness that the two waiting groups hoped for opposite verdicts. But I no longer thought or wished in words. By this time, fear had stopped any coherent thoughts.

After many hours, the family and friends of the accused suddenly began moving toward the courtroom door. At the same time, Lucy walked briskly toward us and announced, "The jury has reached a verdict. Let's go back into the courtroom."

A hollow silence filled the room, interrupted only by an occasional light, hesitant cough from the gallery as Lucy, Robert, and I took our seats. I glanced to my right where the defendant's mother sat. Her face, like mine, revealed nothing. I no longer sensed the presence of Andreas's friends and their parents; they had disappeared on the benches behind me. Anticipation and dread filled my heart, and a chill ran through my body. We sat in silence, awaiting the arrival of the judge and jury.

"All rise!" The bailiff's voice erupted out of the silence to honor the entrance of the judge and jurors one last time. The hands of the large square wall clock at the front of the room read quarter after three.

"Please be seated," instructed the bailiff.

After we all sat down, the judge gave permission to the clerk to take the verdict slip from the jury foreman.

"Mr. Foreman," the clerk said, "has your jury agreed upon its verdict?"

"It has," the juror resolutely replied.

"May I have the verdict slip, please?" the clerk asked the foreman. After taking the slip, the clerk continued addressing the foreman. "Mr. Foreman, in regard to this indictment against Corey McCale, what say you? Guilty or not guilty?"

"Guilty," the foreman answered, his single word carrying the power of a tsunami as the weight of the verdict spread across the room in undulating waves.

"Guilty of what, sir?" the clerk inquired.

"Second-degree murder," responded the foreman. Audible gasps rose from spectators in the gallery.

"Oh, no!" cried out Mr. Harris, his face flushed crimson. The attorney purposefully lifted his arms and protectively placed them onto Corey McCale's back. As he pulled away from his young client, Mr. Harris let his chest and arms fall to the defendant's table with a heavy thump.

I turned my head and saw the group of women surround the mother of Corey McCale as she let out heart-wrenching screams, the kind of screams that had exploded from my soul in that windowless hospital room after the young doctor announced, "Andreas gave up his fight for life this morning at quarter past ten."

As I stood with my husband and wept, I silently asked myself, *Why am I crying? This is the verdict I wanted and needed to hear.* Trembling, I realized it was their pain now. I had already lost my son forever.

The judge banged on his gavel and shouted, "Order in the court!"

Once the spectators were silent, the clerk continued, "Members of the jury, you have rendered the defendant guilty of murder in the second degree. Is that correct, Mr. Foreman?"

"Yes, sir."

"Judge, may the jury be polled, please?" Mr. Harris requested.

As the clerk asked each member of the jury how he or she had voted and each one answered, "Guilty," I couldn't stop shaking and found myself barely able to stand. Throughout the past few days, just to survive, a flickering flame deep within me had sensed that this trial could not have been real, thus the horror of the reality had not reached the depth of my whole being. But now the guilty verdict extinguished that flame. The crime and the trial were real. My soul had heard the truth. Andreas wasn't coming home. Overwhelmed, I methodically moved my eyes from one juror to the next, hoping my gaze would reflect the gratitude I had for their service, for bearing witness over the past seven days to my child's murder. On the occasions when our eyes met, I felt like they were wordlessly telling me, "I heard your son's pain. What happened to him was wrong, inhumane. Neither he nor you deserved his fate. The dangerous person who killed Andreas and caused so much pain must be locked up so that he'll never hurt another person again."

After each member of the jury was polled, the judge once again rapped his gavel and said, "You may be seated. Members of the jury, it's a difficult task, a difficult duty that you have undertaken. You are now free to go, and you may speak to whomever you wish. You are dismissed with the thanks of the Court and the people of Middlesex County for executing your duties so faithfully. It is customary for the judge to speak with the jurors after the verdict, so I will be glad to meet with you in the jury room."

As we rose for the jury one last time, I forced myself to stand up and withhold my tears. Robert and Lucy stood next to me. My thoughts raced on as the jurors left the courtroom. *This is the defendant's sentence, not mine. Why do I not feel relieved? Why am I still shaking? Maybe it's because the verdict confirms that what we've heard during the trial about Andreas's final moments is real and will forever remain real. Nothing will ever change that—ever! We were not in a play, and all the atrocities, the horror, the knife broken in two, Andreas's screams, his pain, his blood on the street and on his clothes, the police—all of that is true. It really happened. I will never wake up from this nightmare and return to the life I had before. Never, ever again. That young man standing before us in the pin-striped suit is the one responsible for all this horror—him and the violent culture in which he grew up. All of this is the truth! It's real! Andreas is dead. He will never get parole. His father and I, his brother, his grandparents, his uncles, aunts, cousins, and friends—all of us must go on without him. We'll all go to our graves without ever sharing another smile with Andreas. We'll live the rest of our lives remembering the reprehensible acts of the murderer who took Andreas's life.*

After the jury exited the room, Mr. Rapacki declared, "The Commonwealth moves for sentencing, Your Honor."

"Very well, then," the judge replied. "The sentence being mandatory and required by law, the clerk will now pronounce the sentence."

"Corey McCale, the Court sentences you to a term of life in prison. You have the right to appeal the sentence imposed this day," the clerk stated.

"Bail is revoked. Mr. McCale will now be transported to the Department of Corrections for incarceration." With a final bang of his gavel, the judge proclaimed, "Court is adjourned."

In his oversize jacket, the young murderer stood facing the judge as two tall police officers walked toward his table. With his mother still sitting in the gallery, he quickly turned around to face her. *Will he beg for her forgiveness before they take him away? Will he tell us how sorry he is?* As the two officers moved closer to him, he thrust his right hand into his suit coat and hastily pulled it back out, forming a fist around something he'd retrieved from his pocket. Startled by the glint of metal, the image of him clutching a large kitchen knife in his hand flashed through my mind as he extended his arm and violently threw the object toward his mother. A ring of keys crashed at his mother's feet, eliminating any hope I'd had that he might feel some small amount of remorse for what he'd done to Andreas.

I focused on the two officers swiftly taking hold of the young man's hands. The back of his pin-striped jacket creased as they bent his arms upward. He made no sound as they cuffed his hands together. My body cringed, and guilt rushed into my heart. *Aren't we adults ultimately responsible? Did we let him down? What did we do wrong that we didn't help him grow up into a law-abiding young man?*

I stared at the eighteen-year-old convicted murderer, an officer on either side of him, as they headed toward the metal tomb that opened behind the judge's seat. I couldn't help but see a fleeting image of Andreas's motionless body lying in a sage-green, satin-lined coffin, his beautiful hands—dependable, tender, and strong—forming a cross over his chest.

Epilogue

As contrary as it sounds, after the trial, my grief intensified. Hearing the word *guilty* over and over from one juror to the next, then witnessing my son's murderer being handcuffed and escorted away, made the truth of what had happened to Andreas utterly real. The part of me that would come home each day after trial hoping to find Andreas resting on his bed had been forever extinguished.

After the sentencing, on October 6, 1989, Robert, Tom, and I had no choice but to learn to live with our new reality. Each of us continued to cope as best we could. Robert immersed himself in his work; Tom went back to UMass Amherst to continue his undergraduate studies; and I spent much of my time either working or attending the homicide support group. I continued to journal as it was a connection with Andreas that allowed me to express and sort out my emotions. Still, sometimes there were no words for what I was feeling, and in our family and close network of friends, everybody was hurting.

At this point, life was devoid of Andreas's physical presence and filled with the pain of his constant absence from our family life. This feeling was especially intense when the three of us were together at home without him, his room empty. So much had been lost. Never again would we celebrate birthdays and holidays or simply share Sunday dinners as a family of four. We would not see Andreas graduate from college, develop a career, or perhaps find a life partner and have children. It seemed surreal that so much could've changed for the three of us while the world continued to spin and life around us went on as usual.

Nine months after Andreas's death, I traveled to visit my parents who lived in a small village near Frankfurt. I was still so emotionally raw at the time that thoughts of Andreas were constant. One day, I'd taken the train into the city, and as I wandered along the main avenue, I suddenly felt compelled to turn down a narrow, cobblestoned street. Both sides of the street were lined with shops of all sorts: a little café, a hardware store, and a clothing store for women. As I passed a small bookshop housed in a flint-gray stone building, a sudden and intense compulsion led me through the store's entryway and directly to a clerk. Asking the young saleswoman if she might have any books on grieving the violent death of a loved one, she led me through rows of stacked books until we came upon a neat pile next to a small window. Pulling a slim white paperback from the stack, she said in German, "Maybe this book will be of interest to you."

Scanning the cover, my heartbeat quickened. I took a deep breath, trying hard to keep my hands from shaking. Struck, I reread the title: *Suddenly and Unexpected: Memories of Andreas Who Left Us Much Too Early*. Flipping through its pages, I came across journal entries written by the father, mother, and brother of a boy who was accidentally killed while crossing a city street. The authors' words expressed feelings that I'd come to know intimately since my Andreas was murdered. The book spoke directly to my heart, and I held it tight as I paid the clerk and walked back out onto the bustling street.

Not long after reading about "their" Andreas, I reached out to the Carl Heinz-Ulrich family, the authors of the book whose pain, grief, and confusion mirrored my own. The letter I received in response has been by my side ever since. "There is no answer to why," they wrote. "How about asking ourselves for what purpose?"

Since then, over the many years, I have been continually surprised by similar synchronistic experiences. It's like impalpable energies have been guiding me to certain places, people, and things to comfort me.

Is it something my aching soul is seeking? Am I being reminded that I'm not alone? Who is with me? Is it God and/or the spirit of Andreas? While these occurrences have not diminished my pain, they have helped me feel less alone and go on with my life.

I still remember the morning I woke up having heard in my dreams the sound of a booming male voice with a German accent exclaiming, as if coming from deep within the earth, "Here is Professor Tillich! Here is Professor Tillich!" The urgency of the voice, along with a vague sense that I might've seen or heard the name before, stirred my curiosity. Later that day, I felt compelled to go to our local library to see if they had any books by or references to a person with that surname. The helpful librarian led me to a short row of books all written by Paul Tillich, who, I would soon discover, was a widely regarded German American philosopher and theologian.

Feeling a bit stunned that the voice in my dream had led me to this place, I first stood in silence. Letting my hand reach randomly toward the shelf, curious but without any specific expectation, I retrieved a light gray book with green lettering on its cover, which spelled out the title: *The Courage to Be*. Allowing the book's pages to randomly fall open in my hands, to my astonishment, the book opened exactly to the page that explained the words *anxiety* and *fear*—words I had found difficult to differentiate. Later that day, I bought the book, sensing its title had a message for me, and, indeed, I felt fortified to go on, to face what I must and to keep writing.

As the years went by and with the trial well behind us, our family continued to face great challenges. Corey McCale, though convicted by a jury of his peers, continued to deny that he was responsible for Andreas's death. He filed for an appeal, which involved his attorney continuously intruding into the life of one of Andreas's close friends who had testified at trial. Those actions and the ongoing uncertainty added more anxiety to our already heavy hearts. Eventually, in early 1997, the convicted murderer's attorneys filed a motion for a new trial. Thankfully, in March of 1999, almost ten years after the guilty verdict, the court of appeals denied the motion.

Time passed and I continued to struggle with grief. Sometimes I just wanted life to end because the living of it was simply too hard to bear. It was through this struggle that I found myself in a psychologist's office. It was large and warm as natural sunlight streamed in through oversize windows. Bookshelves lined the walls, and a curious iron bar hung above a fireplace. In one corner stood a potted weeping fig tree, a few of its leaves, brown and dead, scattered on the floor at its base. Soon after arriving, a composed man with thick wavy hair that had been casually cut to fall slightly below his collar greeted me with a smile that exuded serenity and calm. Then he gestured for me to take a seat in one of the rattan swivel chairs that stood next to an antique coffee table. After a brief introduction, I asked him whether he knew anything about homicide. He firmly answered, "No." Surprised and struck by his honesty, I immediately made another appointment.

As I left the psychologist's office that first day, I had an inner vision of a forked road and heard a voice from deep within myself say, *Stay with the guru.* I had come to a crossroad and could no longer continue as I had. Although I didn't know it at the time, this was the beginning of a new and critical journey for me. It turned out that this psychologist knew much about our psyche and dreams. I quickly learned to pay attention to my dreams and to experience their images. And over time, I began to glimpse that besides my overwhelming pain, there were deeper parts within myself that still wanted and needed to live. I often saw Andreas in my dreams but in places other than our familiar surroundings. I sensed that he was still with me in spirit, and he continued to let me know that I needed to speak for him, to give words to what happened to him and to our family.

Knowing Andreas's murderer was in prison and hoping that any additional appeals would be denied, I gradually began to participate in dance classes of mainly earthy Latin rhythms and invigorating movements. This helped me reconnect with long-buried aspects of my Venezuelan life. Thinking back, I can now see how listening and moving my body to those deeply imprinted sounds of my childhood helped me bear the pain of both Andreas's continued absence and my own and my family's completely changed lives.

I continued to pay attention to my inner stirrings. When I was feeling close to despair, I would give in to the urge to take long walks without a specific plan or destination. At times, I'd find myself in a bookstore, standing in front of a book that had some meaning for me. At other times, I would enter a church where the sound of someone playing the organ soothed my pain, or I'd visit a park and admire the shape and textured bark of tree branches and the various hues of colorful leaves. At those moments, I felt Andreas with me, reminding me that beauty still exists in the world and that I must carry on so we might both have a voice. I also knew I had to be there for Tom and for our family. I owed my life to sacrifices that my parents—survivors of World War II—had made, and, for my spirit's sake, I needed to create some meaning from what had happened to Andreas.

My early work with that first psychologist proved to be invaluable. His recognition of the depth of my suffering and understanding of my acute traumatic grief reaction contributed greatly to my emotional stability. But despite all the new ways I was learning to cope, I continued struggling to accept the cruel and violent way Andreas had been ripped from our family, and I despaired at living life without him. This eventually prompted me to continue my journey with a second psychologist.

Like the first psychologist I saw, this new clinician had much knowledge about the psyche, dreams, grief, and trauma. With patience and dedication to our work together, he helped me recognize and reclaim my own strength. To this day, I still feel deep appreciation for all he helped me discover in myself. Never once did he say, "You have to move on Christine. You have grieved enough." Instead, I remember how he sat with my pain and listened with his heart. In this way, I was able to keep working, continue focusing on this memoir, and deal with the many adjustments my family was making in our daily lives.

At the end of April 2003, four years after Corey McCale's request for a new trial was rejected and two years before he became eligible for parole, I unexpectedly received a neatly handwritten letter from him. Needless to say, it shocked me to my core. I rushed over to Betty, a member of my homicide support group whose daughter Anne was murdered on her way to her twenty-third birthday party. Betty shared my horror as we studied the letter, trying to understand the intent behind it. *Is he sincere? Why now?* we asked ourselves.

It took me a year to respond, but on May 3, 2004, having been moved by the letter in which he finally admitted his guilt in Andreas's death and expressed torment as a result of his actions, I listened to my intuition and, perhaps naively, wrote back to Corey McCale. While I hoped his motivation in reaching out to me was truly unselfish, I knew that he would be eligible for parole that year, after serving fifteen years of his sentence. It was impossible not to be suspicious of the timing of his letter and long-awaited admission of guilt. I couldn't help but wonder whether he was hoping to smooth the path toward probation and an early release. I hoped that wasn't the case. I hoped that by contacting him, I would learn what made it possible for him to commit such an atrocious act and find out if his remorse for killing my dear son was sincere. I had many questions that needed answering. I also hoped that by engaging with him, he might gain some insight into his own behavior and, therefore, would no longer be a threat to society once released.

Corey McCale's first parole hearing came on August 25, 2004. I awkwardly exchanged glances with the prisoner as he entered the hearing room. By then, the two of us had already exchanged a few letters. Addressing the parole board, I read my victim impact statement. "I cannot imagine that the one who took my son's life will walk the sidewalks that Andreas used to walk, will breathe the fresh air, and see the sky and the birds that he loved so much, while Andreas remains buried, dead forever," I began. "I worry that if he walks out from behind the prison walls, constant fear will once again permeate my life, my remaining son's life, and the lives of Andreas's friends. What can Corey McCale say to us to calm those fears? I would strongly suggest that he remain in prison at least until all of us can bear the reality of seeing him walk down the streets and not become engulfed by fear."

As I listened to the parole board members, one by one, remarking on one of the "most dangerous inmates we've had in a long time, or ever," they detailed the transgressions of his behavior behind bars during the last fifteen years. After everyone was done speaking, one of the board members asked the prisoner, "Would you let a person with that behavior out on the streets?"

Without hesitation, Corey McCale replied resolutely, "No." I was impressed with his quick and honest response.

Over the next three years, Corey and I continued to correspond. Having expressed my fear of him in my impact statement at his first parole hearing, Corey wrote to me, reassuring me that he was in the process of changing. In his letters, he said he'd made a promise to me and to Andreas to become and remain nonviolent. Knowing that softened my heart and lessened my own fear. It seemed to me that his letters from prison became increasingly honest as he responded to my questions and talked about his struggle to change. He began to reassure me more firmly that he was committed to a life of nonviolence.

I had noticed that our written correspondence helped soften the intensity of the rage I felt for what he had done to my dear son. In some mysterious way, through the trust he placed in me by telling me about his troubled life and my heart's willingness to hear his true feelings, I could not help but see his humanity. That helped me become less fearful and better prepared for the second parole hearing, which was scheduled for August 28, 2007, and his possible release from prison.

On that day, I again read a victim impact statement to the parole board. In it, I expressed my concerns that change takes time. I felt it was too early to know whether Corey McCale was strong enough to withstand the pressures of life outside prison. His family was at the hearing too, advocating for his parole. They had come ready with clear suggestions for a plan following his release.

Ultimately, parole was granted. As we left the hearing, Andreas's friends, who on that last night of his life heard his screams and saw his blood spilled on the street, were in shock. Although on some level I had anticipated that Corey would be granted parole, I was also shaken and angry at the continued pain his release would inevitably cause Andreas's brother and friends. My own pain stemmed largely from knowing that what once was could never be again. Because of the death sentence Corey McCale had imposed on my child, Andreas would never come home again.

In the aftermath of such an enormous loss, Robert, Tom, and I did what we had to do to survive, while never forgetting Andreas. I have learned that there is no right or wrong way to react to traumatic loss. We could only grieve in our own ways, follow our own hearts, and do what we had to do to cope and carry on.

Some years after we lost our son, Robert and I went our separate ways. He continued his career and, eventually, remarried and expanded his family. Tom finished his university studies, earned a law degree, and became an attorney in the Boston area. For a few years following Andreas's death, I continued my work with youth in the nearby public school system. In 1992, I accepted a position as a clinical social worker at an urban community health center, where I remained until 2016 when I retired to devote myself to completing this book. My heart's insistence for me to tell our story had become impossible to ignore.

Tom and I still occasionally meet with Mike, Todd, Tim, and Brian. We talk of our lives today and share memories of our beloved Andreas. I am deeply fond of these men, now all in their early fifties, and proud of what they have done with their lives. My heart swells with gratitude for their steadfast friendship and devotion, even in death, to Andreas. I still live in the home in Belmont where Robert and I raised Tom and Andreas and am blessed that Tom and Andreas's closest friends remain nearby, making our visits possible.

From my earliest journaling with letters to Andreas in the immediate aftermath of his death through the many drafts of this book, the passage of time and the process of putting my feelings to paper have eased sorrow's painful grip on my heart. Emanating from a once dark and grief-stricken place, my soul's numinous energy has become stronger now that my pain has found expression. Shining brightly at times, its loving light cuts through the cloud cover of loss and heartache.

To all the visible and invisible companions who have guided and supported me over the years, I am thankful beyond words that Andreas has spoken through us. May others find hope and comfort in our story.

Andreas's light lives on.

Remembering Andreas

I'm deeply moved by the ways in which my family, our friends, and Andreas's and Tom's friends have let me know that they still miss and love Andreas. I find great comfort in reading the letters and cards many of them have sent to me over the years. Andreas still is, and always will be, in our hearts and in the memories we share.

In 2008, nineteen years after Andreas was murdered, I received a letter from his friend Brian Walsh, who was with him on the night he was killed and later testified at the trial:

> Christine,
> I lay in bed this morning at 1:00 a.m., thinking about a lot of stuff when it struck me that the date was June 11. I instantly began thinking of Andreas. Shortly after that, I heard a noise in my condo that I'd never heard before and thought maybe it was him saying hello because I was awake. I have thoughts like that all the time and try very hard to only remember the fond moments we shared while he was here, like the trips to the quarries in Gloucester for a day of fun with the guys and the countless trips we took in Tom's Trans Am because Andreas loved those types of cars so much.
>
> I laugh when I remember the battery in the car from his grandmother going dead before he was even old enough to drive it because we spent so many nights sitting in it while it was parked in the garage. I like to think that adopting Andreas's

"gentle giant" attitude has made me a more reasonable and less agitated adult, and I have his memory to thank.

All these thoughts are a nice way to keep Andreas with me for the rest of my life. My thoughts are also with you and your family at times like these because I know you think about him every day, and days like today must be much more difficult.

My thoughts are with everyone who was touched by Andreas's gentle nature and caring personality. I know how much they must miss him like I do.

—Brian

In March 2017, almost twenty-eight years after Andreas's murder, I received a letter from Mike Driscoll after sending him an early draft of this book. Like Brian and Todd, Mike was with Andreas the night he was stabbed and beaten to death.

Hi Christine,

Thank you for sending over the manuscript. I think it speaks volumes about your courage and strength that you put so much time and energy into it in the hopes, as you put it, "that it may help someone else."

I often reference the experience of that night and the ramifications, whether it's in parenting my own son to avoid violence and situations that can lead to tragedy or in counseling a wayward young man at work who might think beating someone up is the answer to a disagreement.

I continue to miss and love Andreas, and I think about him daily. Turning his memory and what happened into something positive feels good and right. Thank you for promoting that and providing us with an incredible example. You are truly one of my heroes.

Take care,

—Mike

Todd Giles, another of Andreas's closest friends, spent the last Saturday afternoon and evening of Andreas's life with him. I remember feeling a sense of peace that afternoon listening to the boys' laughter escaping through the bedroom door as they sang along to Tom Petty's "Free Fallin'" and Bob Seger's "Against the Wind." When I met with Todd in 2012, he told me, "Andreas always had a lot of friends. Everybody wanted to be around him. He's still the closest friend I've ever had. We were instantly drawn to each other from the moment we met during our freshman year of high school. It was his easygoing nature and quick humor that made it fun to be with him. Plus, he was very adaptable to whomever he was with. I was surprised at Andreas's maturity and that he liked Gary Wright's "Dream Weaver," which was considered an old song by our teenage standards.

"I'll never forget when he showed up with a perfectly drawn map of the road where I was stopped by a police officer who'd accused me of some traffic violation," Todd continued. "Without any hesitation, he went with me to court to contest the ticket, even showing up with the map he'd drawn of the area where this supposed infraction took place. Thanks to his map, I was able to explain to the judge the exact way I was driving. I firmly believe the judge dismissed the charges thanks to Andreas's precise drawings."

In 2019, after reviewing the manuscript for this book, Todd wrote to me again.

Dear Christine,
It's been thirty years and I still think about Andreas all the time. I'll hear a certain song or drive by a memorable spot that reminds me of him, and he'll just pop into my head as if he's trying to get my attention. We were the best of friends and spent countless hours together. The pain I feel from losing Andreas has never faded. He was one of a kind, and I cherish the memories we had together. I also look back and realize how naive we were at that age.

At nineteen, we thought we were invincible, but I learned very quickly how fragile life is. Now, as a parent of two teenage sons, ages thirteen and fifteen, I can't even imagine how you felt and still feel as Andreas's mother. His death was a tragic event for everyone involved, and I feel somewhat responsible for what happened—we all do. That night, there were so many opportunities along the way; if any one of us had questioned what we were doing, maybe the outcome would've been different. As an adult, it's easy to say that, but looking back to being a nineteen-year-old, we couldn't see that there were real consequences to the actions we took. This book is a great way to honor Andreas's life, and I think you have spoken for him perfectly. I'm sure he is very pleased.

—Todd

Andreas playing with his older brother, Tom, in the yard of our home in Belmont, Massachusetts. (Summer 1970)

Andreas at the wheel of his and Tom's toy fire truck.

*Andreas staying warm in a sweater knitted by
his New Jersey Oma as he sits on the bleachers
of Glacken Field. (Autumn 1971)*

*In the spring of 1972, we traveled with the boys
to Venezuela to visit my parents. It was the first
time that Oma and Opa met Andreas. Here, Tom
(left) and Andreas play with their Matchbox cars
in the yard of my parents' house in the city of
Maracaibo. A giant sandbox for two toddlers!*

*Clearly delighted with the result of their efforts, Tom
(age 7) peeks out of the driver's side "window" as Andreas
(age 5) pops his head through the "sunroof" of their
homemade cardboard automobile. (Spring 1975)*

Making a stop at the water pump near their New Jersey Oma and Opa's cottage along the shore of picturesque Schroon Lake in the Adirondacks. Tom (left, age 7) holds on while Andreas (age 5) works the pump. (Summer 1975)

From left to right: Andreas, Robert, and Tom celebrating Tom's eighth birthday in June 1976.

From left to right: Jürgen, Tom (age 8), Robert, and Andreas (age 6) happily horsing around on our living room rug. Jürgen, my eldest brother, was visiting from Maracaibo, Venezuela. (Late summer 1976)

With Tom (age 9) at the wheel and Andreas (age 7) in the passenger seat, the boys "try out" their Uncle Jürgen's parked Camaro on a visit to Venezuela in August 1977.

Andreas (age 8) paddling with Tom (age 10)
on Schroon Lake. (Summer 1978)

My graduation from the University of Massachusetts in 1979 with a bachelor's degree in sociology. Celebrating with me are (from left to right): Jürgen, my mother, Andreas (age 9), Robert's mother, Tom (age 11, wearing my cap and gown), me, and my father.

From left to right: Andreas, me, Tom, and Jürgen
on my graduation day. (1979)

In July 1980, we celebrated the fortieth wedding anniversary of Robert's parents, whom Andreas and Tom referred to as Oma and Opa from New Jersey. From left to right: Robert, Oma, Tom, Opa, Andreas, and me.

To celebrate their fifth grade graduation and the end of their elementary school days, Andreas and his classmates took a trip to Cape Cod. This was his first outing away from home without family. (Late spring 1981)

Taking a break along the route of a bike tour with friends during the summer of 1983. The two-hundred-mile journey took Robert, Tom, Andreas, and their friends Mark and Peter from Acton, Massachusetts, through Vermont and into eastern New York. They stayed at youth hostels along the way to their destination: Robert's parents' summer place in the Adirondacks. From left to right: Robert, Mark, Andreas, Peter, and Tom.

*Andreas and me on the campus of Smith College
in Northampton, Massachusetts, following the
graduation ceremony where I received my master's
in social work in the summer of 1984.*

From left to right: Tom, me, and Andreas on the campus of Smith College on the day I received my master's degree.

Tom, Andreas, and Robert in our dining room, celebrating Andreas's sixteenth birthday on January 24, 1986.

Andreas at the bow of a motorboat as he enjoys a summer day on the waters off the coast of Maine with friends Mark Haley (left) and Todd Giles (center). (June 1986)

Following Andreas's graduation from Belmont High in 1988, we had a small backyard party to celebrate this milestone. Here, Andreas poses for a "formal" photo that I took of him.

May 14, 1989, would turn out to be the final Mother's Day I'd celebrate with both Tom (left, age 20) and Andreas (age 19). How could we know that just three weeks later Andreas would be taken from us?

Sunday, May 14, 1989, our final family photo. Andreas (center) stands tall in front of the blooming dogwood tree in our front yard. From left to right, he is flanked by Robert, me, my father, my mother, and Tom. My parents, who'd made a transatlantic trip from their small village in Germany so we could celebrate Mother's Day together, had no idea this would be the last time they'd see Andreas.

Although it's a bit out of focus, I like this candid snapshot of Andreas. Surrounded by friends and classmates, relaxed, and holding his new high school diploma at his side, he looks over his shoulder and smiles back at Robert, me, and Tom. (June 1988)

*A stone engraved with Andreas's name rests
among the names of a multitude of other homicide
victims at the Garden of Peace in Boston.*

Acknowledgments

First of all, I need to thank the strong survival spirit I inherited from my mother's family, who were farmers in eastern Germany for generations until they were forcibly displaced at the end of World War II, and from my father who, against all odds, survived the war and brought us to a foreign country to start over again. By teaching us the importance of persistence and hard work, he became a role model to me and my brothers. I also want to acknowledge the universal, life-giving spirit whose presence I came to recognize more clearly in the wake of Andreas's death.

I thank my eldest son, Tom Dresp, for not giving up on life and for holding steady under the crushing pain of having to move on without his younger brother and only sibling. We both noticed that, too often, crime stories focus on the perpetrator, while failing to convey the depth of pain and suffering victims and their families endure. In his quiet way, Tom encouraged me to keep writing from the perspective of the victim's mother.

I am grateful to Andreas's father, Robert Dresp, who, despite his own pain in the wake of our son's death, somehow managed to continue working full-time to support our family. This allowed me to take a leave of absence from my job and write the first draft of my manuscript.

In addition, I would like to recognize several people who have stood by me since I began this endeavor. Most of them have graciously taken the time to read my manuscript and offer valuable support, feedback, and encouraging words. Lucy Murray-Brown was assigned as our family's victim advocate shortly after Andreas's death. Her guidance and support proved critical in shepherding us through the grueling murder trial and beyond. Over the years, she has become a friend who often reminds me that Andreas's goodness and light live on. I also want to thank Lucy's husband, Jeremy, for his suggestions for the book's title.

My former colleague Barbara Holleman, who majored in English during her undergraduate studies, kindly offered to read my first draft, even though I had no intention of turning it into a book at the time. She carefully scribbled her emotional reactions in the margins, which made me realize the impact my story could have on others. As Barbara gently nudged me to pursue publication, she never balked at reviewing yet another draft. I have no words to express my gratitude for her friendship and encouragement.

My friend Martin La Roche has often noted the importance of making my story available to a larger audience. Martin's generosity and unwavering support have been invaluable, but most of all, I thank Martin for his friendship.

From the moment I met my colleague Iris Zaki when I returned to work after Andreas's death, she became a dear friend and accompanied me in my quest to reconnect with other aspects of life. Iris helped me balance my sorrow while learning to reclaim the joy of dance and music and helped me see that the larger world continues to exist even after a horrifying loss. No matter how many days I disappeared into my "writing cave," Iris was always there to join me again to face the world.

Thank you to my friend Irene Firenze, a fellow social worker who helped me transition into a new life without Andreas. With Irene, I embraced the beauty in this world outside my grief as we hiked and enjoyed the mountains and the sea.

I also want to thank Bette Spear, director of the OMEGA Bereavement Support Program and facilitator of the homicide support group

I attended for more than a decade. Bette provided me with a safe place to meet other mothers, fathers, sisters, brothers, sons, and daughters of homicide victims. Her caring and support—as well as that of my fellow group members Evelyn, Betty, Jane, Lynn, Helaine, Todd, his wife Judy, and others—have sustained me throughout the years.

I'm greatly indebted to my former colleagues at the community health center where I worked for twenty-four years. They whole-heartedly supported my need to write by allowing me to take a leave of absence to focus on the first draft of my manuscript. I also want to recognize Mary Lyons Hunter and Pedro Garrido-Castillo for reading and commenting on the manuscript.

Thank you to Mopsy Kennedy. It was in her class, Writing from Your Own Experience, that I first read out loud a piece on how it felt to lose Andreas to murder. I'm grateful to Mopsy and my classmates at the Cambridge Center for Adult Education for their comments and valuable feedback.

I met Linda Leedy Schneider at the 2010 conference of the International Women's Writing Guild. Linda is a poet, writing coach, psychotherapist, and a fellow clinical social worker who also tries to convey human emotions through the written word. Linda became my writing mentor, and after reading my manuscript, she said, "I want to teach you how to make it stronger." Her sensitive guidance helped me develop my manuscript into this book.

In 2013, I had the opportunity to attend a writing seminar at Harvard Medical School. There, I was introduced to agents, editors, and other professionals who gave useful feedback after I pitched my work. I would especially like to thank Dr. Nausheen Din and literary agent Albert LaFarge for evaluating my manuscript and encouraging me to make it available to the general public.

Literary publicist Barbara Delage came into my life when my manuscript was ready to take the next step toward publication. Her enthusiasm, validation of my book, and clear, straightforward approach to the project helped me remain steady throughout the arduous task of revising and polishing the manuscript. Throughout the process, I felt her genuine empathy for my loss and her love for Andreas.

Author Sarah Perry, an early reader of my manuscript, provided honest, invaluable feedback. After reading her moving memoir, *After the Eclipse*, I knew she'd be the perfect beta reader for my story. Sarah's input provided clarity and helped my writing along.

I have much appreciation for my editor, Jennifer Huston Schaeffer of White Dog Editorial, who agreed to take on my manuscript. I am particularly grateful for her sensitivity to my voice, English being my third language. I can only express awe at how tactfully and compassionately she approached the subject matter and helped me see places in the manuscript that needed more clarification.

Many thanks to book designer Deb Tremper of Six Penny Graphics. Deb took my initial ideas and sensitively transformed them into a visually striking cover, capturing the essence of Andreas.

Thank you to Cynthia Fraser Graves and Androscoggin Press.

I'm very grateful to Andreas's friends, especially Todd Giles, Mike Driscoll, Tim Killilea, and Brian Walsh, who have steadfastly stayed in touch with me over the years. They continue to remind me how much they still miss and love Andreas and will always remember him as part of their close circle of friends.

Last but certainly not least, I have been blessed with kindhearted and loving family and friends in the United States, Venezuela, Mexico, and Germany, some of whom are mentioned by name in this book. It's hard to find words to adequately convey my gratitude for every one of you and how much your presence in my life has meant to me.

About the Author

Christine Wolf, MSW, was born in Germany in 1945 to World War II refugees. Her family left Germany for Venezuela when she was seven years old. At the age of twenty-two, Christine moved to Cambridge, Massachusetts, after marrying Robert Dresp in Maracaibo, Venezuela in 1967. Christine's two sons, Tom and Andreas, were born in 1968 and 1970, respectively. While raising her sons, Christine earned her bachelor's degree in sociology from the University of Massachusetts in Boston. In 1984, she received her master's degree from Smith College School for Social Work, which led to a long and fulfilling career, including seven years with the public school system as a bilingual clinical social worker and twenty-four years at a community health center. Based on the journals she kept at the time, *Speak for Me, Mom* chronicles her experiences as a mother in the aftermath of her son's murder and during the trial of his accused killer.

Praise for *Speak for Me, Mom*

"A triumph and valuable bereavement resource."

—Lucy Murray-Brown, former victim/witness advocate at the Middlesex County District Attorney's Office

"An electrifying account of a mother's post-traumatic reality. Her perspective is both personal and universal."

—Barbara Holleman, retired clinical social worker

"This book reminds us that a criminal investigation and prosecution can be a further assault upon the living. Provides valuable insights to guide the efforts of prosecutors, victim advocates, and judges as they work through today's needless tragedies."

—Ed Rapacki, Ellis & Rapacki LLP

"A call to action for our mental health system, police, and courts."

—Iris M. Zaki, retired school psychologist

"Helpful to families trying to cope with a tragic death and adults raising adolescent boys. This is a story that needs to be told."

—Todd Giles, a close friend of murder victim, Andreas Dresp

"As the fellow parent of a murder victim, I found myself caught up in this mother's suffering and her quest to make some sense of it all. A gripping read."
> —Betty Borghesani, mother of Anne E. Borghesani (3/27/1967–3/31/1990) and founder of the Anne E. Borghesani Community Foundation

"I couldn't stop reading! The thread of trauma weaving through this book is heart-wrenching."
> —Bette Spear, homicide bereavement therapist

"A mother's raw and haunting tale of the murder of her son and its aftermath. This story stays with you long after you've finished reading."
> —Mary Lyons Hunter, psychologist

"A tender testament to one mother's love and a wrenching account of the impact violence has on both victims and survivors. This book will help others who have been similarly traumatized."
> —Heidi H. White, author of *At the Edge of the Storm*

"Moving and inspirational; a book that's hard to put down."
> —Pedro Garrido-Castillo, psychologist

"As an adult, child, and adolescent psychiatrist with a keen interest in risk evaluations and the aftermath of trauma, I read this captivating book cover to cover in a single sitting. Raw, gritty, and honest, a courageous telling of life-altering events."
> —Nausheen Din, psychiatrist

"A very personal exploration of the many ways that grief and trauma mix with healing after the loss of a child to homicide. This book is a must-read for any parent who has experienced the worst form of loss and for anyone who imagines that there is such a thing as closure."
—Todd McKie, father of Jesse McKie (1969–1990)

"A generous gift to anyone who wants to understand better how the spirit survives following an unspeakable tragedy."
—Irene Firenze, retired clinical social worker

Made in the USA
Middletown, DE
30 October 2023

41543066R00149